The Truth

The Truth About Iniquity

EXPERIENCE

the Joy of Your Salvation

Unlock the Mystery,
Fulfill The Ancient Prophecy,
Cut the Head off your Giant,
and Discover God's Plan for Your Life

A message from Heaven for God's shepherds and His precious sheep

• A Lesson In Fatherlessness •

DR. RAYMOND MARSHALL

ISBN: 978-1-936521-00-5

Published by SparkPub Media, LLC
Tulsa, Oklahoma

Contents

Dedication

First and foremost, I give all the thanks and praise, all the glory to my Lord and Savior, Jesus Christ. I thank Him for revealing this truth. This vital truth is the very nature of who He is to me. I thank Him for saving me, delivering me, healing me, and setting me free from the lifelong prison I found myself in. I am unquestionably free.

Next, I want to give thanks to a particular person. Twenty-three years ago, I met a very special lady in my life, a lady who was to become my wife, Dr. Mary Marshall. Little did I know (at the time) of the importance of our meeting. We began as study partners, became friends and began dating.

One evening, in the fall of 1989, after she returned from attending a leadership camp, she started sharing her experience at the camp. She shared about the activities they participated in and then she began talking about "walking with the Lord." I asked her what she was talking about, as I knew nothing about that subject. She, led by the Holy Spirit, began to reveal God's plan of salvation to me. After hearing about His plan, I prayed with her and accepted and received Jesus as my personal Lord and Savior.

From this start, our lives together were forever changed for the better. For her taking the time to share the truth of "this gospel" I am eternally grateful. I say, "Thank you for being a wonderful wife, friend, companion, mother and, second only to Jesus, the love of my life."

I also want to give special thanks to, at the time of this writing, our four boys. To Isaac, Samuel, Joshua and Luke, I say, "I love you, I enjoy you, and I thank you for your boundless energy, patience, love and joy."

I also want to take this opportunity to thank those who, by their actions, expressed their confidence and support of this vital work. To every person who God used as a father-figure in my live, I thank you for revealing genuine fragments of God's true nature by your attitudes and actions. To all who encouraged me to take the time to write this message down so it can be delivered to others, I say, "Thank you for believing in me and encouraging me to deliver this message." To our precious ministry staff, I say, "Thank you for your full commitment. Thank you for going with us as we've followed the Lord."

Lastly, I'd like to thank the amazing staff of SparkPub Media for helping me bring this message to the world.

Dr. Raymond P. Marshall

Preface

Have you ever faced an impossible situation? Have you ever reached the end of your rope but still feel like you are making no progress and to no avail? Have you ever faced a situation that exists and persists no matter what you do or have done? If so, do you want to know how you can overcome it? Do you want to be enabled to rise victoriously over it? If so, this book is for you. It is the time for your giant to be defeated and silenced.

I have, as long as I can remember, enjoyed solving puzzles, untying knots, and straightening things out. It just seems to have come natural to me. I realize now it is something God has gifted and graced me to do since I was a little boy.

When I am working on solving a puzzle of any kind, one way the Lord encourages and helps me is with what He calls "the big picture." When you get back far enough to see the big picture, you can see where the piece you are working on fits with all the rest and it helps you determine the course of action for your next step.

In order to unlock the mystery of iniquity in your life, the Lord gave me this big picture to help prepare you and enable you to accomplish this task:

He said to me, *"In the beginning days of My church, the church body, the ecclesia, flowed in fullness of revelation. This happened once I poured out my Spirit after the day of Pentecost had fully come. I spoke through Jesus Himself and said "upon this rock I will build My church and the gates of hell will not prevail against it." Then, through years of persecution and the dark ages, satan attempted to steal the church and squelch the revelation of Christ completely. As the four-hundred years of the dark ages began to come to a close, revelation began to emerge and come to light again. With each passing generation, more and more light has been given, each successive generation given the potential to receive more light."*

Through the vehicle of progressive revelation, our ancestors and fathers in the faith have been able to share their experience with us and help in our walk with the Lord. I thank God for everything the elders who came before me were able to share with me. It has been beneficial to stand on their shoulders and not have to re-invent the wheel. However, it was only up to a certain point. Through this revelation the Lord delivered to me, I know and understand, intimately for myself, the other side of this subject as well. Each of our elders, ancestors and forefathers were teaching, preaching, functioning and operating in all the revelation and light they had been given to share with others, and many of them got stopped. Through tragedy, calamity, circumstance, attack or trial, the transfer of revelation got cut off. For some, their lives were cut short and for others, their ministries were hindered, changed and altered. The Lord revealed to me these events were all part of satan's plan to stop the flow of revelation and thwart the plan of God.

When the Lord revealed the truth about iniquity to me and rescued me from the brink of death, I had never heard about the mystery of iniquity or its solution preached, shared or taught by any of my forefathers. None of them had been able to receive or share this vital revelation with me. And, yet, this revelation was the very tool the Lord has used to save my life and deliver me, and now, thousands of others, from a lifetime of torments of all kinds.

This is a fresh revelation from the Lord, Himself. Through the application of this revelation, the Lord will equip you to fulfill your call and restore you as a fully functioning member of the body of Christ.

The Lord told me this: *"As the living body of Christ moves back into the fullness of revelation again, you must keep our eyes off of any man as your source of revelation. You must avoid, as mentioned in the book of Romans 1, elevating the creation above the Creator."* He went on to say this: *"Anything you ever heard through a man that brought you revelation, light, wisdom or direction that worked (that actually made a tangible difference) in your life was from Me. One of the places you have gotten off track is this: Giving a man credit for what I said or by turning an idea I gave into a god. I have always given men wisdom, insight, revelation and ideas in order to help, assist, bless, encourage and strengthen them in their situation, but the idea I give them is just that, an idea. The idea is not a god, and it is definitely not to become a doctrine."* The Lord finished this thought with these words, words which to this very day, are etched into my spirit, *"Don't ever take credit yourself or give another man credit for what I said or what I did, and don't allow a great idea I give you to become a god."*

To further solidify and back up this point, the Lord gave me this scripture:

> *"In all your ways acknowledge Him, and He shall direct your paths."*
>
> Proverbs 3:6 NKJV

The place we must all look to, give credit to and never lose sight of is He who is the Author and Finisher of our faith and the Giver of all revelation. We must keep our spiritual eyes and ears off of any man or idea and keep them on Jesus.

This revelation came about this very way. It came by revelation and it is revelation. Through this particular revelation, God will enable you to unlock the mystery and discover the plan He has for you to do with the rest of your life.

After I received this revelation from Him and its application in my own life, The Lord said this to me, *"Son, My people are dying to know what I told you."*

He added this statement, *"In truth, they are dying because they don't know what I told you."*

Then, He finished with this statement, *"I gave this revelation to you because I knew you would do what I want you to do with it."*

It is for this reason I am writing this book and sharing this message and revelation. I know, practically, through experience for myself with the Lord Jesus Christ, Himself, this message is of utmost importance for you and your family right now, as well as for the wonderful plan and future God has ordained for you.

INTRODUCTION

On Saturday, December 25th, 2010, at 5:30 in the morning, as I began to wake up, the Lord Jesus visited my house. His visit began with a vision and ended with an assignment.

Now, I must tell you, by the grace of God, I normally sleep very well. Prior to this event, I have recalled just a few dreams in forty-two years. With that being said, I can tell you this: To this day I distinctly remember the vision with great clarity and understanding.

In the vision the Lord brought to me and enabled me to see, it appeared as if I was standing in a large auditorium. I observed everything from the vantage point of being behind the curtains backstage, looking out into a large auditorium.

The first thing I saw was the podium on a backdrop of a large crowd of people. After that, I saw myself climb up the stairs to the platform and then walk across the stage from the right side of my visual field to the middle and slowly stop. I saw myself standing with a small group of people. At that particular moment in the vision, one person was speaking to the assembly and another was speaking quietly to me. The next event that happened surprised me.

I saw the person who was speaking introduce me. Then they turned and handed me the microphone. In the vision, while I was standing behind the podium holding the microphone, as I turned my face to the right, I observed the Lord approach the spot where I was standing and I saw Him hand me a scripture.

He handed me a scripture right out of the Bible.

He handed it to me like a baker would hand you a fresh baked loaf of Roquefort and almond sourdough or like a king would hand a sword to a knight who had just been knighted. He handed it to me with such care and precision I knew it was precious, valuable, and to be handled with great care.

Later that cold December morning, I shared this vision from the Lord with my wife, Dr. Mary Marshall. She had slept in a little later that morning because the night before we had stayed up longer than usual setting up gifts for our boys around the Christmas tree. She asked me if I had written down what the Lord had shown me. I told her, "I did. I looked the scripture up and I wrote a few things down I feel the Lord revealed to me."

The rest of the day we spent celebrating Christmas, exchanging gifts, cleaning up wrapping paper, enjoying our boys, laughing, playing and later in the day, having dinner. The next week was also pretty normal, you might just say—routine—as well.

Eleven days later, however, on January 5th, The Lord re-visited me and dropped something into my heart that I had never thought about before and I will never forget. His word to me was, *"This revelation I am going to give you is one of the major keys why my people can't and won't do the plan of God for their lives. Why My people, people I have chosen, called, and anointed can't and won't fulfill My call on their lives."*

That word He delivered was, at that very moment, etched into the fiber of my being. I will never forget it. The Lord spoke it to me on Wednesday night, January 5th, 2011. As I am preparing this manuscript for the editor, this Word is just as real to me now as it was then. The Lord has tested me on this material and has proven and re-proven it to me and other ministers who have applied it thousands of times since then. Every week we are hearing testimonies from people who have been healed, restored, delivered, and set free through the application of this revelation and message the Lord delivered to me.

When He spoke this word to me, I had finished listening to a live worship service that was broadcast into our home. I had just gotten the family snuggled into bed after the service, when, as I was walking through the house to the kitchen to get a drink and a snack, the Word of the Lord came to me. After receiving this Word, I said, "Lord, every person in the Body of Christ needs to know about this."

At that point, the Lord clearly said these words to me, "*This revelation is not just for you, son, but is for all My children.*" I knew then I had the great honor, responsibility, and privilege of presenting this God-given revelation to His children—those who, as He said, have been unable—many who are and have been living their lives literally paralyzed, with their lives and gifting completely on hold. As a result of the paralysis, many of His children have not been able, are not currently able, and will not be able to do the very things they were actually created by Him and sent from Heaven to do.

Three days after the Lord delivered this message to me, a friend and patient we have helped take care of for about ten years called me and we met for lunch. He had been speaking to Pastor Roy Evans, the Senior Pastor of Northstar Church in Pryor, Oklahoma. He had mentioned to Pastor Roy that "the Lord has spoken to and encouraged me through Dr. Ray, and it would be a blessing if you would have him come to the church and speak to our church." My friend told me Pastor Roy had prayed and he felt impressed of the Lord to have me come. During the lunch visit that Tuesday, my friend asked, "Would you come?" I replied, "I'd be happy to. The Lord gave me the message."

The very first testimony of what the Lord did through this revelation happened to me, personally.

That cold winter night, I studied in depth what the Lord had brought to me. I gathered together different references, Bible translations, dictionaries, encyclopedias, as well as commentaries. In short, I got a focused, concentrated, and thorough education (like the beginning preparations for a doctoral thesis) about the subject The Lord instructed me to study.

Now, at this point, you may ask, "What happened to you?" I can tell you without any reservation what I experienced. Just in the study of the material and appropriating the truth of this revelation to my own life, the Lord completely delivered me from sixteen years of re-occurring heart-attack symptoms, fluttering and skipping heartbeats as well as the awful symptoms of diabetes I had dealt with since I was thirteen.

I had been for years noticing what felt like a choke-hold around my neck, shortness of breath, restriction in my chest and neck, fluttering and skipping of my heart as well as a condition called diabetic ketoacidosis, a condition indicative of diabetes, in which the person has a very strong pungent odor that emanates from their body.

Then, immediately after activating this key to this hidden covenant promise, they were all gone. The chest pressure was gone, the breathing restriction left, the fluttering and skipping stopped. I remember distinctly the very next day, while taking a truck ride, saying to my wife, Dr. Mary Marshall, "I do not remember ever being able to breathe like this." It was the most pure, clean, refreshing breath I had ever breathed. It was like I could not reach the bottom of my lungs. They were absolutely clear and free. I was fully functioning and breathing completely without any restriction. In addition, about a month later, it just dawned on me, I realized I no longer had that strong, pungent odor emanating from out of my body.

I also began to become acutely aware of something else. I had heard from others who had been in the presence of Jesus, Himself speak about this, but had never experienced it for myself, until that very moment. I became acutely aware of an unmistakable heavenly fragrance. It began to exude from every part of my being. As it came through my skin, it felt like a very fine lotion or oil. Everything I touched smelled of this fragrance. Everywhere I went, I noticed this wonderful fragrance. This fragrance filled my house, my car, my office and every place I went. It even filled the hospital room of a loved one who we visited in the hospital. That marvelous heavenly fragrance was on me, with me and around me everywhere I went.

I know now I touched heaven and heaven touched me that very night. Jesus reached out His hand to mine and I reached out my hand to Him. In the process, He touched my body and made me completely whole.

When I was asked about speaking to the assembly I remember saying these words, "I am so excited! I can't wait to come! God gave me the message!"

I was honored and privileged to share this pure, unedited, and unadulterated message, straight from the throne room of heaven, to the precious people of the Northstar Church congregation.

We shared the message on January 26th, 2011, and again, the Lord confirmed His Word by performing signs, wonders and miracles in the lives of the people in that group of believers.

This testimony from the meeting is of a young lady who had come to the meeting place for a very different purpose. One year prior to the meeting, her husband had committed suicide.

He had taken his life right in front of her.

She had tried many things to get past this painful event, but to no avail. She was not a believer, but she thought she had committed the unpardonable sin. No matter what she did, the forces of darkness that had driven her husband to commit suicide would never ever leave her. She decided to come to the location where we were meeting that very night with the intention of taking her life. (She was completely unaware of the meeting happening that night until she arrived at this pre-determined location for her suicide attempt).

The demon who had driven her husband to commit suicide the year before had driven her to the very same place on the night of this meeting.

However, just before the meeting, a member of the church walked by her car, invited her inside, and at the end of the meeting, at the very moment we prayed and appropriated this revelation I am sharing with you today, the Lord completely delivered her from that demonic spirit, saved her, delivered her from methamphetamines and other drugs as well as healed her right shoulder. The Lord completely snatched her from the jaws of death.

Many others reported being delivered from the pain of divorces, failed businesses, loss of loved ones, hurts caused by friends and acquaintances, ruined relationships and many other painful memories from their past, and then were enabled and equipped by the Lord to get back into His plan for their lives. All of this without years of counseling, tedious and time-consuming instruction and expensive doctor's appointments.

After the meeting, I knew I wasn't finished, but just getting started. Not only did I experience the results myself, but I witnessed the results in hundreds and now thousands of others' lives. I witnessed the genuine, real, tangible experiential fruit multiply in the members of that congregation and to many others since then.

In one of our most recent meetings, the Lord again moved and powerfully touched the people gathered in the assembly. One of the most notable points I remember was this: Not one person in the meeting acted like they wanted to leave. I believe the Lord literally touched each and every person in the meeting. Then, after this particular time of refreshing in the presence of the Lord, this wonderful testimony came forth. At the end of the meeting, after leading the gathered assembly in the prayer to appropriate this promise in their lives, immediately, the Lord confirmed His word right in front of our eyes.

One of the first people to come forward and testify was a lady who came up to my wife and spoke these words: She said, "You'll just never know. You'll just never know. My son was murdered. I have been bound by that horrible spirit for years, but now I am free! You'll just never know."

I believe and declare this word, His word, is for you and all who will hear it and apply it in their lives. And, to further clarify, I am not talking about some future time. I am referring to right now. I believe this Word will literally, as it did for me, save your life. This is the reason I am writing this book. You not only need to know about this revelation, but you also need to know how to appropriate it in your own life. You need to know how to take full advantage of all God has done for you, so you can completely fulfill His call on your life.

I believe strongly in my heart the Lord wants to minister to you, speak something specific to you and He desires to do something very special, both in you and for you, as you receive and appropriate the truth of this revelation for yourself.

The message of this book can be condensed to these four very significant words that the Lord gave me: "*Forgiven, Pardoned, Prepared, and Filled.*" These words very accurately describe the gifts God has given to equip and prepare us for everything He has called us to do.

As you read these words, I pray the Lord will use each and every word in such a way that His Word and His revelation will come forth clearly, boldly, effectively, accurately, and concisely.

Dr. Raymond P. Marshall

CHAPTER ONE

God Has a Plan

As I wrote earlier, it was a cold January night in Branson, Missouri. I was sitting on my couch very, very quietly, desperately seeking the Lord's Wisdom for what I should do about the heart attack I was having. It was extremely critical I found His wisdom for the situation I found myself in, so I began desperately seeking the Lord what I should do. Immediately, He reminded me about the vision He had brought to me in December, so I started my study right where He led me, with the scripture He handed me in the vision.

I started my urgent, life-saving study with Jeremiah 29:11.

As I began to read and meditate on the verse He gave me, this thought dawned upon me: *"Doc, My Word is clear about My plan for your life."*

The following translations of the verse the Lord delivered to me will leave no doubt in your mind to the truth of this statement. The Lord impressed upon me this truth as well: It was and is very important for me to know this, and as He shared it with me, I knew it was also vitally important for you to know and understand this as well—He has a wonderful and glorious plan for your life and every one of us are necessary parts. We all have an integral role, an absolutely essential part, of His glorious plan.

Listen to this.

> *For I know the thoughts that I think toward you, saith the LORD, thoughts of peace, and not of evil, to give you an expected end .*
>
> Jeremiah 29:11 KJV

In the margin of my Bible, the Hebrew of the words *"expected end"* are translated as *"the end and expectation."* So knowing God's heart about your life will give you hope for your future. Knowing God's heart about you and your life will cause you to expect Him to do something good for you.

The following Bible translations of this verse bring further light to that promise and give you hope. Hope that you can believe what God tells you, Hope that you will believe what God tells you and lastly hope that will enable you to not just to believe, but to believe to see, to experience all God has promised come to pass in your life.

> *For I know the thoughts and plans that I have for you, says the Lord, thoughts and plans for welfare and peace and not for evil, to give you hope in your final outcome. (AMP).*
>
> *For I know the plans I have for you, declares the Lord, plans for welfare and not for evil, to give you a future and a hope. (ESV).*
>
> *I alone know the plans I have for you, plans to bring you prosperity and not disaster, plans to bring about the future you hope for. (GNT).*

Did you notice, in that last translation, He said, "I *alone* know the plans to bring about the future you hope for?" It is something he alone knows.

Not your mom, not your grandmother, not your grandfather, your father, your brother or sister. Not your rabbi, your pastor or even your best friend or spouse. Not the devil or any of his cohorts or any people who yield to him. Your Father God alone knows it.

Since He alone knows it, the more time you spend with Him, in His presence, the more revelation you will receive (from Him) regarding His plan for your life.

Once He begins to reveal His plan, He will start to show you steps to take. He will start giving you the instruction and grace to know and do what He asks you to do. It's really that simple. It will work this way at the beginning, throughout the middle and for each and every step you make along the way. It's something He alone can do and will do.

Now, let's look at another translation of that same verse:

> *I know the plans that I have for you, declares the Lord, they are plans for peace and not disaster, plans to give you a future filled with hope (GW).*

With that idea fresh on your mind, have you ever thought about God's plan for your life? Have you ever wondered why you don't know what His plan is? Have you ever wondered why you can't or won't do the thing you know is His will for your life?

After the Lord gave me this scripture, I began meditating on it for myself. I also thought about the many people I have met and seen as patients in our office over the years. As I thought about their various situations and histories and I thought about God's plan for each of our lives, the Lord said this to me:

"The plans for evil, the plans for disaster, any plan that ended in you getting injured, suffering loss, death or destruction were not part of My original plan. These are part of the curse in the earth left behind by Adam's sin. A curse is not a blessing in disguise. A curse is a curse and a blessing is a blessing, and I alone have the ability to take the curse, turn the curse and use the curse you have experienced, are experiencing, and may experience to unearth an awesome, wonderful, powerful and major blessing in your life. I alone have the ability to enable and equip you to overcome whatever type of curse you are facing or will ever face."

Let me read to you the characteristics of God's thoughts and plans for you:

GOD's plans are:

- Plans that bring you healing
- Plans that bring you restoration
- Plans that bring you peace
- Plans filled with hope
- Plans filled with expectation
- Plans for your provision
- Plans for your future
- Plans for your welfare
- Plans to bring about the future you hope for

Then the Lord said it to me again:

"I alone have the ability to take the curse, turn the curse and use the curse you have experienced, are experiencing, and may experience to unearth an awesome, wonderful, powerful and major blessing in your life. I alone have the ability to enable and equip you to overcome whatever type of curse you are facing or will ever face."

Now, with that in mind, let's get back to the revelation the Lord delivered to me. On January 5th, 2011, around 10:30pm, the Lord spoke to me. I had just tucked my family into bed for the night and was walking through the house to get a drink of water. As I was walking through the living room, the Lord spoke to me in my heart just as clear as a bell.

Did my ears hear it? Did my eyes see it? No, but on the inside of me I heard it. He asked me this question, *"Son, did you know there is a difference between sin and iniquity?"*

I said, "I never thought about them being different, never even considered it. In fact, every time I had seen the two words written in my Bible before I thought they were the same. The first time I read the word "iniquity" in my bible I thought it was just a different name for sin and thought it may have been just a King James-Elizabethan English phrase."

He asked me again, *"Doc, did you know there's a difference?"* He said it with so much authority I knew I must check it out. There was a very distinct sense of urgency in His question to me.

CHAPTER TWO

Iniquity Defined

I quickly decided to act on what He told me. The situation I was in and the symptoms I was dealing with were alarming, to say the least. I remember getting situated into a position on the couch that was fairly comfortable (as comfortable as a person can be in the beginning stages of a major heart attack, so I will just say fairly-comfortable). Then I said, "Yes Lord, now that You mention it, I do notice that."

When the Lord poses such a question to me, I have found it is best to find out what He's talking about. He would not ask me the question unless it was important.

I started by looking up definitions, studying different translations, as well as all the other information I could find. I had a mobile Smartphone in my possession that night, so it made the matter a bit easier. I looked up the definition in Vine's, as well as in the Bible encyclopedia and searched the entire Bible for the term "iniquity" in multiple translations so I could see how it was used in context.

In summary, I found out the word "iniquity" has several different meanings, but the one the Lord had me focus on for this study is the Hebrew word "avon." This word, "avon" in Hebrew and "iniquity" in English are the very same word as the word "unrighteousness" found throughout the Bible. The Bible also uses another word that often denotes a similar meaning, the word "wicked." The word iniquity/avon often denotes a similar meaning as the word "twisted." The definition of iniquity also says it is a bent or a twist. It also includes and incorporates the idea of a stamped impression, like what happens when a person hammers patterns into leather. To bring further clarification, the word iniquity has a very similar definition to another word, the word "mark" mentioned in the book of Revelation 19 where it mentions people who received the "mark of the beast."

Like the term "iniquity," the word "mark" means:

1. a stamp, an imprinted mark

i.e. the mark stamped on the forehead or the right hand as the badge of the followers of the Antichrist

2. the mark branded upon horses

3. thing carved, sculpture, graven work of idolatrous images.

Iniquity is also directly related to another term, "punishment." When something is marked by iniquity, it has been set apart and designated for destruction and punishment. The term iniquity also carries the meaning of something molded, twisted, perverted or distorted (like modeled clay). The last description of iniquity in the Bible encyclopedia said it denotes the character of the sin and as such is distinguished from sin.

The Lord said to me, *"A lot of good people have equated iniquity and sin, but they're not the same."* In fact, the Lord revealed to me this truth: satan had, through the vehicle of deception, hidden iniquity under the guise of sin, and as long as he can get a person to think the two are the same subject (and handled the same way), he gets to work them over and continue to wreak havoc in their lives at his will. It gives him, literally, completely unhindered access into a person's life.

This is part of the truth the Lord clearly revealed to me: and I am sharing with you.

Sin and iniquity both individually and distinctly need to be dealt with.

Now, so we can further differentiate them, a sin is a temptation acted upon, a committed act, a transgression of God's laws, whether committed by yourself or committed against you that violates the principles of God's kingdom that results in you being estranged or separated from God.

Iniquity, on the other hand, is the resulting condition of estrangement or separation. It is what happens to you or someone else in the area of the soul as a result of the sin or transgression. It is the effect of sin. There is literally a spiritual substance (iniquity) that gets deposited in you and on you every time you sin, every time there is a transgression and every time you ever get hurt. Iniquity causes your soul to get stamped, bent, twisted and distorted. This is the very substance that, once deposited, cracks, twists, distorts, injures, and affects you in your soul.

The Lord then gave me this example: *"If you step into soft mud, your foot will create a depression, a rut, a footprint as evidence that you stepped in the mud. The action of the foot stepping in the mud is the sin or transgression. But the depression, the rut, the footprint, the evidence that's left behind is the iniquity."* He went on to tell me, *"There is only one fix, only one solution for iniquity!"*

For a child of the living God, the fix, the solution for iniquity is part of our covenant, it is something God made provision for, but, as we have begun to see, is something He alone can do. In addition, unless you know about the fix and how to appropriate it, you can go your whole life carrying iniquity on your person. It will, through the lack of revealed knowledge from God, affect your entire life.

The Lord then said, *"So many people are trying to deal with that issue (iniquity) themselves, without My help, and they are not making any progress in their lives. As a result, they keep wandering, they keep going around the very same mountain again and again and again—essentially, they are making wasted movements. They are moving without making any forward progress in their lives. Not only that, but their problems are multiplying. More mountains, more challenges, then more vain and useless wandering."*

To further clarify this point, the Lord led me to Ezekiel 16:49. The word iniquity in this passage is the very same Hebrew word avon, as mentioned above.

> *"Behold, this was the iniquity of thy sister Sodom, pride, fullness of bread, and abundance of idleness was in her and in her daughters, neither did she strengthen the hand of the poor and needy." (KJV)*

Yes, you read it right...pride, fullness of bread, abundance of idleness, not strengthening the hand of the poor and needy. These were not the sins of Sodom and Gamorrah, these were the footprint, the fruit, the result of the sins and abominations that occurred there. It was literally the iniquity from the sins and abominations that marked those places for destruction with fire and brimstone.

You read earlier that God has an amazing wonderful plan for your life. He had a great plan for Sodom and Gomorrah also. Do you know what are some of the biggest challenges are to being able to do the plan of God for your life?

Satan's plan and our misguided plans.

And, the Lord showed me, as they relate to iniquity, just how those two misdirected plans created the damaging unpleasant memories and experiences from behind you, from your past. And not just your past in general, but specifically, the parts of your past connected with the negative experiences that injured you.

Now, most everybody knows about sin and most everyone knows about asking God for forgiveness, but iniquity, however, is completely different from sin. Iniquity is the RESULT of sin. It is the FOOTPRINT of sin. It is the damage left behind from sin. It is the evidence left behind after the sin encounter. To make matters worse, every sin, transgression or hurt has a certain amount of iniquity that accompanies it. Iniquity is the hidden silent partner to each and every sin, each and every transgression and each and every hurt you have ever experienced.

In the book, I Samuel 2:30, is written this phrase: *"Those who honor Me, I will honor."* In this instance, you honor the Lord by accepting and receiving what He did, by receiving His free gift. It's a heavenly gift from our Father God. He gave us a gift that provides the way for us to deal with iniquity. It is something that is instrumental in preparing us to do what He has called us to do.

As a result of this God-given revelation, the truth about iniquity is being fully exposed. Finally, by the grace of God, iniquity is now able to be completely dealt with and permanently eliminated from our lives.

CHAPTER THREE

The Source of Iniquity: Uncovered, Discovered, and Located

As my late evening study session that cold January night in Branson, Missouri, continued to evolve, pressure began to mount on my physical body. It was much like what I had experienced off and on over the past sixteen years, but the intensity of the attack this time was much greater than I had ever experienced before.

In the middle of this very pressing situation, the Lord had me look at another group of scriptures, Ezekiel 28:14-16.

In this chapter, the prophet Ezekiel brought the Word of the Lord to the prince of Tyrus. He was the man in the leadership position in this province. While this message was brought by a man who was speaking to a man, the words and description given to him by the Holy Spirit also let the reader know the Word of the Lord is making reference to satan, as he, in God's original plan was the anointed cherub that God chose and created to cover His very throne in Heaven.

We see this truth in verses fourteen and fifteen:

> *You were the anointed cherub that covers with overshadowing [wings], and I set you so. You were upon the holy mountain of God; you walked up and down in the midst of the stones of fire [like the paved work of gleaming sapphire stone upon which the God of Israel walked on Mount Sinai]. You were blameless in your ways from the day you were created until iniquity and guilt were found in you. (AMP).*

I said to the Lord, "Since iniquity is the footprint and the result of sin, then satan, just like the prince of Tyrus, must have sinned." The Lord quickly responded to me and said these words, *"Read the very next verse."*

Verse 16:

> *Through the abundance of your commerce you were filled with lawlessness and violence, and you sinned; therefore I cast you out as a profane thing from the mountain of God and the guardian cherub drove you out from the midst of the stones of fire.*

Right there was his sin. The iniquity found in them (satan and Tyrus) was the result of this very sin.

The sin was taking their eyes off of God and putting them onto monetary gain. The monetary gain they obtained by the abundance of commerce mixed with lawlessness and violence. In other words, their sin was unjust gain.

The Lord then said to me, *"That is why I told you to never do something just for money. Make your decisions based not on finances and money, but rather make decisions based upon how they will affect your ability to help people and how they will affect the people you minister to."*

He went on to say to me further, *"If you make the mistake of doing something just for money, you will open yourself up to what satan (and Tyrus) did before he got cast out of heaven (and just as it was in the case of the prince of Tyrus, he got removed from his God-chosen, God-appointed position.)"*

As I thought and meditated upon what the Lord just showed me, this next scripture came with force up to my mind *"You cannot serve God and mammon (money)." (Luke 16:13, Matthew 6:24)*

Not only that, but the Lord brought something else to my attention.

He asked me, *"Did you notice the presence of iniquity immediately disqualified him (satan/Lucifer) from My plan?"*

I just knew in my heart at this point there had to be a plethora of information about this subject throughout the Bible, so I dug in.

CHAPTER FOUR

How Iniquity Affects God's Kids

At this point of the study, I was still sitting, propped up on the couch. I was still trying to decide what I was going to do. As a doctor, I am well aware of different symptoms and what different symptoms mean. I was becoming more and more acutely aware of the medical fact that I was in the middle of a massive heart-attack. I was trying to decide how I was going to get to the hospital and still have my family taken care of as well as other responsibilities. At the same time, I also became more and more interested to find out and see what the Lord wanted to show me about iniquity. I wanted to see how iniquity affected His kids, so I began to choose to pay less attention to the heart-attack symptoms and began to look further into what the Lord was showing me. I began to search even more diligently throughout the Bible in multiple translations. I started thoroughly searching the scriptures for the complete truth about iniquity.

I found many different scriptures regarding iniquity, and one, after the next, after the next, after the next, the puzzle pieces began to make sense and come together. The big picture began to emerge.

The first scripture the Lord showed me immediately began to shed light on the subject:

> *If I regard iniquity in my heart, the Lord will not hear me.*
> Psalm 66:18 KJV

Have you ever prayed and wondered why an answer didn't come?

I have.

Have you ever attempted to communicate with God, but could not discern His voice?

I have.

Have you ever attempted to discern the voice of God but His voice was muted, silenced, absent or unclear?

I have.

I had every one of these experiences happen in my life.

Each and every time a circumstance happens like this, it erodes your faith and confidence a little more.

If these things have happened to you, this is an issue that needs to be addressed. Now, just to re-iterate, as we saw earlier, iniquity is not sin; it's the footprint of sin; it's the effect of sin, the result of sin, whether you committed the sinful act or someone committed the act against you.

I do not know about you, but I know about me.

Just after reading one scripture, I had all the motivation I needed to get all the iniquity out of my life. I want the Lord to be able to hear me and hear my prayers.

With this piece of knowledge, I had the first little spark of hope. I remember saying this to myself, somehow I knew, "If I keep looking, He'll show me more."

In this next scripture, you'll see a second witness to the above mentioned truth:

> *But your iniquities have made a separation between you and your God, and your sins have hidden His face from you, so that He will not hear.*
>
> Isaiah 59:2 AMP

As you can see in this scripture, sin hides God's face from you, but iniquity causes a separation (a space or distance) between you and your God. After a sin or transgression occurs, you can seek God and ask for forgiveness and immediately His face is turned toward you, but you are still separated (distanced) from the presence of God. In this place of separation, it is nearly impossible to discern and hear the voice of God clearly.

Another spark of hope and encouragement shot through me, urging me to continue.

The Lord then said, *"Let's look at the book of Job."*

I asked Him, "Can anything good come out of the book of Job?" [I heard many people talk (as well as read commentaries) about the book of Job in the past, and none of them were very encouraging].

He said, *"Yes."*

In the course of this study, the book of Job is where a good portion of the information regarding this revelation came from.

In Job 10:14, it says, *If I sin, then You observe me, and you will not acquit me from my iniquity and guilt (AMP).*

We see again that sin and iniquity are connected, but are two completely different subjects and must be handled differently.

On one hand there is the sin, the act that God observes and then, on the other hand there is mark left behind from the sin or act, iniquity. Iniquity creates a spot, a mark, a stamped impression, the footprint. It marks you for destruction. It causes you to feel the guilt, the shame, the condemnation. It also causes you to experience all the emotional turmoil that was associated with the sin, transgression or hurt. Iniquity is the issue that determines the length and severity of your prison sentence. It connects you spiritually with the consequence and the penalty for the sin or transgression or hurt.

Of course, as we look at scriptures in the book of Job, we must remember Job did not have an intercessor, someone to take the place and stand between God and judgment, someone who stands between God and the penalty for the sin, but thank God, we do.

Let's continue our study with Job 11:14, God gave these instructions: *If iniquity is in your hand, put it far away and do not let wickedness reside in your tent (NKJV).*

At this point I asked the question, "How do you do this? How does a person get rid of iniquity?"

The Lord clearly revealed to me this truth: "*Since the truth about iniquity and it's solution have not been being preached and taught, it (getting rid of iniquity) is something many people have been unsuccessfully attempting and trying (and trying and attempting) to do themselves, through works, by trying to do it with their own strength (as a work of the flesh) without My help. And, since it is a work of the flesh, it is profiting them nothing."*

But, then, just to reassure me, He told me this, *"I made complete provision for it in My Word and it is something only I can do."*

When He revealed the key to His provision to unlock this mystery, when I actually saw it, when it became a living Word to me and not just a dead letter of the word, I said, "This is absolutely amazing! And every believer in the Body of Christ needs to know about it!"

The Lord replied, *"They do, but, know this: The religious (Pharisees and Sadducees) are going to oppose you until their death and adulterers and adulteresses will chase you down to try to steal it for themselves!"*

The Lord then elaborated: *"Spiritually, forgiveness of sin and the removal of the penalty and the power of the sin, the elimination of the consequences of the sin and their power over your life, are completely different subjects, and must be handled differently."*

He went on to say, *"Forgiveness restores relationship, but the removal of iniquity restores nearness, closeness, intimacy and fellowship."*

CHAPTER FIVE

CAUSE, EFFECT AND INIQUITY

The Lord then said to me *"These subjects (sin and iniquity) directly parallel what you do in your office every day."*

I thought about it for a few moments and said to Him, "You are absolutely right."

Every day in our office, we see people who have had accidents or injuries which have misaligned their spines and cause them to have certain symptoms. The symptom—the pain, the dysfunction, the doctor's report, the diagnosis—is the thing that's talking to them. It's the thing that has their attention.

Without that pain, dysfunction, doctor's report or diagnosis, they could and would be doing great. But the symptoms of the problem are not what we treat. We look for and treat the cause of the symptom. We go for the root cause of the problem and eliminate it. After that, the symptom, the pain, the dysfunction, the bad doctor's report or diagnosis... The effect of the misalignment... Goes completely away. It is wonderful to see people recover from all types of conditions.

This is what happened to me when I was first born. Because of the trauma of my birth, I ended up on a respirator, having seizures and not breathing on my own. After I was born, intervention was done, correction was made and I got off the respirator, stopped having seizures and started breathing on my own. I got my life back. And every day, we get to help other people get their lives back. There is nothing more rewarding than seeing someone else get their life back. That way they get back into life and do what they were made to do.

Down the line, avoiding other injuries is great and that's wonderful, but when a trauma occurs and misalignment results, you must do what you need to do to get your body back into its proper place if you want all your body functions to be restored back to the way God made them to be.

The best way that I can describe it to you is the way the Lord described it to me. He said, *"Doc, the specific thing that I've gifted and graced you to do is to help get the body back into the place I made it, so it will function the way I created it."*

We are not the Healer, and we tell every person who comes in to receive care that we are not. God has graced us. He has anointed us. He has called us to do the type of work we do. The Lord is with us. By His grace, call and the anointing on our lives, we get to see Him perform miracles through what we do every single day.

As a side note: As you take care of those around you and minister to people, one of the primary areas you want to always focus on is to establish, create and maintain an environment, an atmosphere where the Lord is honored; A place where His choices are respected. The Lord toid me this truth: Only He can meet everyone's needs. In an environment where He has free reign and room to move, everyone's needs will be met. That way, He will be able to touch His people in just the way they need.

Once the environment is right, you can focus on what you do best. You can focus on your gifts. The Lord then revealed to me this truth. The grace, anointing and calling He has on each and every one of our lives all come into their fullness as a result of appropriating this key, this covenant promise. This is the very key I am sharing with you in this book.

Through this very same key and revelation, He supplies all the grace and all the anointing needed for you to successfully accomplish all He has called you to do.

Now, back to the revelation. Here is how it parallels what we do.

Regarding the spine:

An accident tears the ligaments that hold the segments of the spine together and causes the spine to misalign. The misalignment compresses the openings the delicate nerves flow through and causes the symptoms the person experiences.

Regarding iniquity:

The sin, transgression or hurt traumatizes the joining between parts (individuals) of His body and causes the iniquity (the twist, the bent, separation or distortion in the soul). The presence of iniquity forces a person to feel the guilt, the shame and all the feelings related to a traumatic event. It also brings back the memories of hurtful situations and causes you to experience (and re-experience and re-experience) a dreadful, fearful, miserable, debilitating circumstance. Left alone, it will become like Goliath. It will actually become a giant in a person's life.

Iniquity makes a spot, a wrinkle, a mark, a stamped impression, a footprint. It marks you for destruction. To reiterate, once iniquity is present, its presence causes you to feel the guilt, the shame, the condemnation, as well as the emotional turmoil that is associated with the sin encounter or hurt. It is the issue that determines the length and severity of the prison sentence. It connects you spiritually with the penalty for the sin, transgression or hurt you suffered and keeps you locked in bondage and prison.

Just like when a person comes in who has a misalignment in their spine, until the misalignment is corrected, the situation and symptoms will not get better, but only worse. It is the very same way with iniquity. If iniquity is not dealt with, it will continue to squeeze and choke the very life out of the person (more and more and more) until they are finally evicted from their body. Not only that, but if the iniquity is not dealt with, it has the power, and most certainly will affect generations of people.

CHAPTER SIX

Storms, Ruts, and Remembrance

The Lord then told me, *"Now, let's go further into the subject of our study, the iniquity, the footprint-the depression in the mud."*

All of us know that storms of life come. Every person who has ever lived on this earth has experienced storms or may be dealing with one right now. So we are all well aware that storms come and go in our lives.

Let me ask you this, where does the run-off from a storm go?

Storm run-off flows all the way down into the ditches, into the depressions and drains and if there is an alteration in the landscape it goes right down into the footprint. It flows right down into the places where there has been disruption in the shape of the surface landscape.

Storms caused by weather conditions pass, and storms of life also pass, but they leave their mark (you know the storm went by because of the evidence) in the ditches, in the depressions, in the footprint. In all the areas affected by iniquity.

With that in mind, the Lord had me look at Job 4:8: It says, *"Even as I have seen, those who plow iniquity and sow trouble reap the same" (NKJV).*

The Lord then led me to look at what is written in Hebrews 9 and 10, which speak about two different sacrifices.

Hebrews 10 talks about the annual sacrifice of bulls and goats performed in the remembrance of sin. It explains in vivid detail this truth: The annual sacrifice and remembrance actually heightened everyone's awareness of their sin and it went on to verify this truth: This type of sacrifice could never and can never take away people's sin.

I said, "Lord, why is that important?"

He said, *"Every single day, people are unknowingly remembering their sin and plowing up the iniquity."*

I said, "Lord, show me."

And because I'm a doctor, He said, *"What is a 'member' to you?"* I said, "It's an arm or leg or an appendage." He said, *"What would happen if you dismembered somebody?"* I said, "You would take off their arm." He then asked *"What would happen if you re-member that arm?"* I said "You would reattach it, re-connect it, and put the arm back into its place and position."

He said to me *"That would be like the annual sacrifice of bulls and goats and the remembrance of sin."* Every year those people re-membered their sin. They got re-connected with it. They re-hashed it. And in doing so, they plowed up the iniquity.

It's no wonder the whole Israelite nation was having issues. Every single hurt, challenge, transgression, or offense they had faced or caused was never wiped out. Instead, just the opposite happened. It was brought into the light and exposed. Instead of moving forward in their lives, every person's heart, feelings, and emotions were plowed up each and every year. And to make matters worse, this event was repeated, much like a dreaded family holiday party or a family get-together, year after year after year.

The same thing happens when the enemy inspires someone (especially those closest to you) to remind you repeatedly about your past failures, your past sins, the laundry list, the list of mistakes that goes back to the first time you met as well as the record of all your wrongs. When the person does that, they (through the vehicle of lack of knowledge) are actually yielding their mouth to satan. He is actually using their mouth to plow up old iniquity and is helping the enemy keep you in bondage.

Side note: The Lord reminded me, *"Any time you (or someone else) try to make another person feel bad, guilty or ashamed for anything they have truly repented of and asked forgiveness for, you have left the ministry of the Holy Spirit."*

Have you wondered why the two-million Israelites couldn't go into the Promised Land? Or why they couldn't fulfill the plan of God for their lives?

The Lord said to me, *"Through the working of iniquity, the enemy was continually able to take them back to the first grade, around the same mountain again because the iniquity was plowed up again and again and again."*

I then asked the Lord, "Do You have any scripture for that?"

He said, "Yes." He then led me to Hebrews11:15.

If they had been thinking with [homesick] remembrance of that country from which they were emigrants, they would have found constant opportunity to return to it. (AMP)

This kind of remembrance will force you to return (perpetually) to the place you were in bondage and slavery. It will return you to the very place God delivered you out of.

The Lord then reminded me of an experience I had when I was small. I was running on the playground to get a kickball that had been kicked so I could get the person "out" before they scored a run. I took off running at full speed after that ball but then heard someone call my name. I looked back, but kept running and encountered a four-inch pole. BONG!

I had the experience that day, but what I learned from it is this: when you are going forward in life, never look back.

To support this thought with scripture,

1 Corinthians 13:5-7 in the *Message* translation says it this way:

(Love) doesn't keep score of the sins of others,
Doesn't revel when others grovel,
Takes pleasure in the flowering of truth,
Puts up with anything,
Trusts God always,
Always looks for the best,

Never looks back,
But keeps going to the end.

The Lord then finished this train of thought with this statement, *"If you want My power to flow in your life, never look back."*

The application of this key the Lord revealed to me enables you to do this. It enables you to completely disconnect from the negative damaging memories from your past. It will absolutely disconnect you from all your failures and regrets. It will empower you to overcome every time from anything and everything that comes across your path.

At this point, as I was thinking about the "remembrance" subject further, The Lord also led me to Ezekiel 21:24, which gave me the final motivation I needed to want to eliminate and eradicate iniquity from my life.

> *Therefore thus says the Lord God: Because you have made your guilt and iniquity to be remembered, in that your transgressions are uncovered, so that in all your doings your sins appear—because, I say, you have come to remembrance, you shall be taken with the [enemy's] hand. (AMP)*

I said it earlier, after the very first scripture I was motivated to get rid of iniquity. Now I became extremely motivated.

Not only was I motivated to live free from iniquity and its effects, but also I became very motivated to make sure I did not plow up iniquity for other people. I do not want to bring up their past sins and failures and do not want to be part of keeping them in bondage. I do not want to be working for the enemy in the lives of any of my loved ones.

Another term closely related to plowing iniquity is the term “Working Iniquity.”

The Lord revealed to me that plowing iniquity/working iniquity is described by these phrases:

- Ripping off the bandage
- Adding insult to injury
- Re-living ones past
- Rubbing it in
- Picking a scab
- Re-hashing it
- Dragging someone back through the mud
- Re-visiting a person’s painful event

To support this matter further, the Lord gave me the very same scripture we just looked at, from 1 Corinthians 13:6 KJV.

(Love) rejoiceth not in iniquity.

Many times, the person doing this, yielding their mouth to the enemy, will say “I’m just playing,” or “I didn’t mean it like that.” Or from the other extreme, “You need to know just how much you hurt me,” or “You are never going to amount to anything.”

Like I said above, not only was I motivated to live free from iniquity and its effects myself, but also I became very motivated to make sure I did not plow up iniquity for other people. I do not want to bring up their past sins and failures and I do not want to be any part of keeping them in bondage. I do not want to be working for the enemy in any way, shape or form in the lives of those I love.

As my thirst for the truth about this subject continued to increase, the Lord then led me to Hosea chapter 4:6-8 as there was a reference to iniquity in the eighth verse:

> *My people are destroyed for lack of knowledge; because you [the priestly nation] have rejected knowledge, I will also reject you that you shall be no priest to Me; seeing you have forgotten the law of your God, I will also forget your children. The more they increased and multiplied [in prosperity and power], the more they sinned against Me; I will change their glory into shame. They feed on the sin of My people and set their heart on their iniquity. (AMP)*

I was being destroyed. I had been dealing with alarming symptoms for years and kept facing the same giants again and again. I had been doing my part in confessing my sin, asking God for forgiveness from past sins and had forgiven others, but was still plagued with the rather alarming heart attack and diabetes symptoms.

As my thirst increased, I was like a starving man standing behind a door with a delicious four course meal on the other side. At this point, the heart attack symptoms were very acute. I felt like I was being squashed by an elephant. The pain and pressure and numbness were going up my neck into my jaw, into my head and down my left shoulder and arm. I was extremely desperate and very, very thirsty.

The Lord then brought to my remembrance (The Lord showed me there is also a good side to remembrance) a scripture in Isaiah 44 where it says:

> *I will pour water upon him who is thirsty, and floods upon the dry ground. I will pour My Spirit upon your*

> *offspring, and My blessing upon your descendants. (AMP)*

I was like that deer mentioned in Psalm 42:1 that pants after the water. I was very thirsty and was crying out to God for a drink.

When I read this above mentioned scripture in Hosea 4 in its context, the Lord revealed His heart to me.

He said to me *"My people are perishing. They are conscious of the hopelessness of their plight already and need to be instructed. Every time you plow up someone's past they have repented and been forgiven for, be conscious of this: you are reminding them about their remitted sins. Make sure you share, train, teach and preach on My way of righteousness. Teach and instruct them about appropriating My righteousness, My peace and My joy in their lives. Teach them what to avoid but do not put all your focus on what not to do. Rather, teach them what to do. Teach them how to live and stay in right standing with Me and with others. Teach them about My kingdom. Teach them how to get free, to live and stay free from sin."*

I reread the whole chapter in context, with specific emphasis at the point in verse eight where it says:

> *They feed on the sin of My people and set their heart on their iniquity. (AMP)*

As I read, re-read, and meditated on this whole passage in context, that night, the Lord spoke gently and specifically to my heart; This revelation dawned on me; *"It (the heart attack I found myself in) is all about the money."*

Over the years, the iniquity related to my past sins, transgressions and hurts I had been forgiven for and had forgiven others for made me feel bad, guilty, and ashamed. It marked me for destruction. It made me feel like I owed everyone something I didn't. Iniquity forced me to throw away and give away personal items I know God had blessed me with. It drove me to overextend myself and provide free medical care to those who I thought would die without my intervention. It made me accept any and every patient and every form of payment plan for our services in the office just so we could get paid. It caused me to not be able to enjoy the best blessings of God in my life, the children God gave me. It consumed my thought life as I searched for a way to get out from under the guilt, shame and condemnation. Giving and throwing these things away was the only thing that seemed to bring a little relief, but it (the relief) was brief and fleeting. It never lasted. In just a few hours (or at the very most, in just a few days) I would start searching for the next thing I could get rid of. I had to find something to give away or throw away so I could get just a little relief from the guilt, shame and horrible heart attack symptoms.

Satan (and well-instructed Pharisees and Sadducees) had deceived me into thinking I was actually acting on the scripture in Proverbs 3:27-28 that says:

> *Do not withhold good from those to whom it is due, when it is in the power of your hand to do so. Do not say to your neighbor, "Go, and come back, And tomorrow I will give it," when you have it with you. (NKJV)*

The Lord showed me, with great clarity, this scripture was referring to withholding good only from those to whom it is due, not to everyone. And He would show me who those were.

He also made it very clear, the only debt I truly owed any other person is to love them with His love. He said this statement to me, *"You don't owe anyone anything except to love them."* At this point, I was a little bewildered. I said, "I don't?" I shook my head. Then He said it again:

"You don't owe anyone anything except to love them."

At this moment, I began to feel hopeful again. And with the hope came a little breath of relief.

As I sat there, dumb founded by how satan (and his Pharisees and Sadducees) had deceived me. The Lord then showed me the instances in the Bible where whole cities had been established and built by iniquity.

The iniquity from people's past mistakes, sins, and hurts made people feel bad, guilty, ashamed and like they owed something they didn't. Whole cities had been built, established and are being run because of unjust gain, guilt, shame and condemnation. They were built, established, and are being run by people bringing guilt offerings. Because of the cause and effect relationship of sin and iniquity and the iniquity not being dealt with, satan has been able to steal church members blind and literally rob them of their God-given inheritance. Working of iniquity has all been part of satan's plan to thwart God's plan and destroy His creation.

The Lord then said to me, *"His (satan's) primary mode of operation is to spread the thing he has, and iniquity is all he has to share."*

He then reiterated to me *"Any time you (or someone else) try to make another person feel bad, guilty or ashamed for anything they have truly repented of and asked forgiveness for, you have left the ministry of the Holy Spirit."* Then, He added, *"Your job is to catch them. My job is to clean them. Don't you try to clean them. That is My job."*

And He finished this subject with this:

"I told my priests through the prophet Hosea to instruct the people in My ways because they (My people) are perishing. They are being made to feel guilty and ashamed for past mistakes and failures they had repented from and have been forgiven for and the resulting guilt and shame is causing them to bring guilt offerings which are filling the church coffers. To the leadership of the church, it appears to be "working" because the money is flowing in and there is a surplus... monetary needs are being met. But at what expense? What is the fruit of money that is coming this way? The fathers are being killed off, the mothers are being widowed and their born (and unborn) children are being murdered, committing suicide and forced into all types of bondage. This is why I have a very dear and precious spot in My heart for widows and orphans. Through the working of iniquity, satan has come into the house of God, deceived the leadership, and My families are losing their spiritual heads as well as their inheritance."

Don't just take my word for it, read Hosea 4 and 5.

You will get a revelation. Not only did I read the two chapters repeatedly in different translations, I read the entire book of Hosea as well.

As I read over these Holy scriptures, not just in the Message translation, but in five other versions, the Lord reminded me of what happened to His people after they created the golden calf. They ended up drunk, naked, and dancing in an orgy around the golden calf. The Lord brought these phrases to my attention in the above mentioned scriptures: "*You* (first My priests and then, as a result, My people) *refuse to recognize the revelation of God.. It's the men who pick up the whores that I'm after. When they (the people) decide to get their lives together and go off looking for God once again, they'll find it's too late. I, God will be long gone. You (priests) have played your sex-and-religion games long enough."*

Just as God used Hosea to originally deliver this message from the Lord, so am I. I am sounding the alarm.

Satan, through the working of iniquity, set his heart on more unjust gain, to attempt to steal God's church, and he has also wowed the leadership and led them to deceive the people to make up calves (religious works, doctrinal errors, religious activities and actions that take the place of God, Himself), to worship these calves they created, and get involved with whoring and prostituting themselves with these calves and idols.

Satan has come to literally steal the church and make it his own.

Satan led them, through the working of iniquity to commit spiritual adultery against the Lord and elevate man, with his ideas, into God's position. This has been his M.O. from the beginning, "I will exalt myself like the Most High."

And as you read above, this focused and pointed attack is directed at the fathers, at the heads of His precious families and churches.

Because of this, many churches have been deceived into choosing, contrary to what Moses did, money and pleasure over the Presence and Power of Almighty God. As result, the priests are not praying between the porch and the altar for the people, the Holy Spirit has been and is being grieved. His holy presence has been removed from many of the churches; the people are not encountering the presence of the Lord. Sinners are not meeting Jesus. Sinners are not being saved and the Lord is not confirming His word with signs, wonders and miracles because His Word ("this gospel") is not being preached. The gospel that is being preached is one that primarily promotes prosperity and self reliance and makes the measure of God's hand being on the ministry be the financial condition of the company. When this becomes the primary measuring stick of the ministry, the ministry has actually been disqualified by the Lord to serve the people of the kingdom. Do not let yourselves be deceived. The love of money is the root of all kinds of evil.

As the Lord is giving me these words, it is 6:28 AM, on Sunday, April 29th, 2012, and as I am typing the words down, in my spirit is resounding the phrase,

"Run (like Joseph did out of his coat) from those who are telling you gain is godliness. Satan has blinded their eyes and bound these folks with perversion, with idol worship. They are bound by the spirit of Baal and cannot see the forest they are in because of the trees. In situations like this, the blind are leading the blind and you both will end up in a ditch. Instead, run with those who are telling you that Godliness with contentment is great gain.

Run from those who put most of the emphasis of how God will bless you abundantly and make you rich and run with those who are telling you that there is a purpose to your prosperity, that God has blessed you, will bless you, and you shall be a blessing.

Run from those places that are just a "God-will-bless-me club" and run with those who are saying that riches and earth-

ly possessions are tools to be used to help others, to assist others, and to promote His Kingdom.

Run from those who tell you to just pray once, call you healed when you obviously are not and then just thank the Lord for answering your prayer and run with those who will pray just like James 5:14 says, just like Elijah and other men and women of God prayed in the Bible.

Run with those who will actually hear from God what to do, what to pray, and how to do it. Run with those who will actually contend with you for the miracle you need. These men and women of God are true men and women of God. They will join with you and persevere with you until the time comes that you are actually experiencing the manifestation of it in your life.

By doing so, you will avoid getting indoctrinated into Baal worship and deceived into thinking that prosperity is the measure by which I am using to show I have qualified the ministry. Instead, measure the qualification of the ministry just like Jesus said you should.

Mark 16, Matthew 24 and Luke 24 say this: The Message being preached (*"this gospel"*) should include (1) *repentance and remission of sin*, (2) will be confirmed with *genuine salvations* where there is tangible fruit of God's conversion in people's lives without extensive counseling sessions teaching people how to be religious and act perfect so they can be blessed, (3) the *Holy Spirit's tangible presence* on the property (He after all IS the Fire of God), and (4) confirmations of the message: *"the Lord worked with them and confirmed the message by accompanying signs."* (In other words, look for the fruit that remains long after the message has been preached). True salvations, his unmistakable presence, signs, wonders and miracles are a must. They have to be there. If they are not, the Lord is not confirming the message that is being preached and He is not with you."

As a further note of clarification, the Lord told me this, *"When I give the message to the preacher and it (My message) is preached, with My voice, it can even be a message on water baptism and I will confirm it with signs, wonders and miracles following." Listen for My voice, not just My words. I said My sheep know My voice. Anyone can speak My words (even satan himself spoke My words) but only those speaking under the genuine unction of My Holy Spirit will be speaking with My voice. My voice is unmistakable and it cannot be falsified."*

Then, He finished with this, *"The measure of the message being preached is the fruit. Instruct my people to look for the fruit. And keep a firm grip on Me. Look for Me to be working among you. This will keep you from being deceived."*

At this point, the Lord showed me a vision of the many people I had met and seen through the years. In my mind I saw people who had family members who died prematurely. I saw wives who had lost husbands before their time; children and grandchildren who had fathers and grandfathers who died too early. I saw young people just starting their lives being murdered. I saw women who had not carried babies to full term and miscarried. I saw teens and young people committing suicide. I also saw the widows and the orphans. I saw all the people who were left behind after iniquity had left its mark. I saw the aftermath of what happened after their passing and the Lord shined His light on satan's operation. *"Kill the shepherd and the sheep will scatter where they are easy prey for the enemy!"*

None of these things just mentioned were ever part of God's original plan and purpose for any of their lives.

God's plan was and still is to restore all satan has stolen.

Side note: As we mentioned earlier, any time you (or someone else) try to make another person feel bad, guilty or ashamed for anything they have truly repented of and asked forgiveness for and teaching people to obtain God's promises and spiritual perfection through works is part of what the Bible calls the "working of iniquity." This is a subject of great importance to the Lord and is mentioned again in chapter 14, entitled "Iniquity and the Return of Jesus."

CHAPTER SEVEN

Iniquity and the Mouth Connection

As I pondered what the Lord had just shown me, literally shaking my head at the magnitude of the revelation the Lord just revealed to me regarding satan's plan to take over His church and the condition of His church, I began to tangibly feel the power of God begin to move over and through my body for somewhere between fifteen and thirty minutes. It was so soothing and relaxing I nearly fell asleep. During this time, I began to feel the heart attack symptoms subside a little and became aware of being able to breathe a little more deeply. I began to get a little relief without feeling forced and manipulated into throwing or giving something away. I began to feel my entire body relax and ease into the beginning stage of relaxation before going to sleep.

As I sat there, feeling the first glimpse of peace, the Lord said to me, *"There is also a strong connection between iniquity and the mouth I want to show you."*

The Lord then had me look at this next scripture in this light, and within it came another major key that all born-again believers need to know, something that alters what comes out of your mouth and completely undermines and negates your God-given ability to speak the words He gives you. It absolutely nullifies the Power of God in and on the words and instructions you receive from Him. As a result, iniquity directs and controls your whole life.

Job 15:5-6 says this:

For your iniquity teaches your mouth, and you choose the tongue of the crafty. Your own mouth condemns you, and not I; yes, your own lips testify against you (AMP).

Yes, you read it right, iniquity, the silent partner of your sins, the iniquity that came through the hurt you experienced, the disappointment you went through, the condemnation you felt and all the emotional turmoil. Iniquity becomes the driving force behind your mouth. Iniquity makes you speak the devil's tongue and makes your own lips testify against you. It causes what you say to fail before the words ever leave your mouth.

It (iniquity) also causes you to say (about your own situation and in your communication with others) what you don't want to say and (as a result) do what you don't want to do.

The Lord showed me, unless you get the iniquity issue resolved, you leave yourself in a place just like the deceased generation of Israelites who did not get to go into the Promised Land—the 2-3 million people who complained, whined, and fussed every single time something came up that they didn't like.

And you know what? That was never God's plan for that generation—never. The whining, griping, complaining, backbiting, and strife were simply a matter of cause and effect (and part of satan's plan for their life).

Now, with that in mind, have you ever been injured or had something happen to you in your life that blind-sided you or was debilitating? Have you ever been injured or injured someone? Have you ever had your feelings traumatized? Has something happened that shook you or damaged you to your core?

The Lord showed me that when you receive an injury or cause an injury, it authorizes satan to bring something from himself (iniquity is all he has) and give it to you.

It (the thing he gives you) then becomes an impediment in your soul. It will actually cause you to speak what you don't want to speak and to do things you don't want to do.

When iniquity is working, it will drive you (and drive you and drive you and drive you) to try to solve your problem by natural means. In other words, by getting myself into the position to receive (self-reliance/self-perfection).

But, thank God, our all-seeing, all-powerful, all-knowing God, the only true and living God, the God who is the God of our salvation. Thank God, He had the foresight to have a plan. In the middle of the heart attack on my body, He revealed His solution to the iniquity problem and I am sharing it with you.

Noting that the scriptures God had shown me up till now were all found in the Old Testament, I asked Him to show me some New Testament scriptures. He directed me to Acts 8, which tells the story of Simon the sorcerer who was trying to buy the gift of the Holy Spirit (which God had given him) with money.

In verse 23, it says, *For I see that you are in a gall of bitterness, and in a bond forged by iniquity to fetter souls (AMP).*

Can you see it? The bitterness in Simon's mouth was being driven by the iniquity. It (iniquity) was also keeping him in bondage, enslaved and completely out of the plan of God.

Paul had told him *"You have neither part nor portion in this matter, for your heart is not right in the sight of God." Acts 8:21 (AMP).*

Iniquity completely disqualified him from the plan of God.

The Lord told me every day this is happening to millions of young people. They have been separated from the presence of the Lord by the cause and effect relationship between sins, hurts and the resulting iniquity. From this place of separation, they are seeking for what they are supposed to do with their life. In this place, they are asking friends, acquaintances, going to career and guidance counselors for advice on a career. They are taking someone else's advice for a career choice, often times deciding on their career based upon the yearly salary they can earn, based on the monetary gain. Then they enter this system by going into debt up to their eyes. Trying to buy the gift only God can give with money.

The Lord told this to me clearly, He said, *"Tell my people not to try to decide what they want to do. Instead tell them to seek Me, seek to know My plan. Then when they find it, get training in that area. That way, you will not be repeating Simon the sorcerer's mistake. You will instead be learning and training yourself in line with that which I have already gifted you to do."*

At this point of my study, I came to this realization, I did not want to be disqualified in any way, shape or form from the plan God has for my life. I also believe none of you want to be disqualified either. I believe you want God to use you in the fullest way He can, so you can do the plan He has for your life.

CHAPTER EIGHT

EXAMPLES OF DEALING WITH INIQUITY

So I asked the Lord, "What do I do? How do I deal with iniquity? How do I help teach others to deal with iniquity so they do not have to repeat the same mistakes?"

The Lord then directed me to Numbers 14:11-12.

As you read these scriptures, please understand this, this group of Israelites' (iniquity-driven) grumbling and complaining finally brought God to the point that He was finished. As longsuffering as the Lord is, He said He was done with that whole group of people.

> *... the Lord said to Moses, "How long will this people provoke (spurn, despise) Me? And how long will it be before they believe Me [trusting in, relying on, clinging to Me], for all the signs which I have performed among them? I will smite them with the pestilence and disinherit them, and will make of you [Moses] a nation greater and mightier than they."*
>
> *But Moses stood in the midst of the Israelites and pleaded with God, saying, "And now, I pray You, let*

the power of my Lord be great, as You have promised, saying, The Lord is long-suffering and slow to anger, and abundant in mercy and loving-kindness, forgiving iniquity and transgression; but He will by no means clear the guilty, visiting the iniquity of the fathers upon the children, upon the third and fourth generation. Pardon, I pray You, the iniquity of this people according to the greatness of Your mercy and loving-kindness, just as You have forgiven [them] from Egypt until now.

Numbers 14:17-19 AMP

Did you know this group of Israelites had been forgiven over and over and over again, yet they still were facing the same old problems? Their yearly sacrifices and remembrance of sins plowed up the iniquity. Iniquity in turn twisted and bent them in their soul, poisoned their mouths and drove them to whine, fuss and complain. Satan's repeated use of the plowing of iniquity eventually disqualified them from God's plan for their lives.

But, on the other side of the coin, let's look what happened when Moses interceded on the their behalf, when he stood in the gap and asked God to pardon them of their iniquity, according to the greatness of His mercy and loving-kindness, just as He had forgiven them from Egypt until now:

"... the Lord said, I have pardoned according to your word."

Numbers 14:20-21 AMP

God did it. He pardoned the iniquity. Now that right there is shouting material!

In my study, the Lord revealed to me in the Jewish commentaries that the entire nation was restored spiritually to the same condition Adam was before he sinned with the forbidden fruit by this simple act of intercession and they remained pure and undefiled until the golden calf incident. One prayer in the presence of almighty God and the entire nation was pardoned from the consequence of every sin they ever committed.

When a person is pardoned, not only is the sin or transgression forgiven, but the terms of punishment, the prison sentence, the record related to the sin or transgression is wiped out. It no longer exists. It's gone immediately.

If you will honor the Lord and receive this gift from Him, He will enable you to live free from the curse that extends to your children to the third and fourth generations and then equip you to follow His plan for your life so your life can be a blessing to a thousand generations.

Do you want to know what happens when a person's sins and iniquities are dealt with?

Immediately, the law of sin and death is cut off. You get snatched from the jaws of death and get catapulted into the plan of God for your life. How do I know? What makes me qualified to talk on this subject? This is what the Lord did for me and I experienced for myself. This is precisely and exactly what God did for me and for my family and for countless other believers as we have shared and applied these truths around the country. Not only that, but from the very day the Lord did this for me and our family, He has used and continues to use our family countless times as a part of the delivery crew for His amazing signs, wonders and miracles.

* As a side note, just to clarify, this group of Israelites had gotten to the point that they had disqualified themselves from God's original plan, so they didn't get to enter the Promised Land. But many other examples from the Bible indicate this truth: After you have the Lord deal with the issue of iniquity, you get instantly propelled back into the plan of He has for your life—**instantly**.

In Psalm 51:1, David clearly explains a good clear example of this: Inspired by the Holy Spirit, he wrote, *"Have mercy upon me, O God, according to Your steadfast love; according to the multitude of Your tender mercy and loving-kindness blot out my transgressions." (KJV).*

The mercy of the Lord is intimately involved with removing iniquity. This Psalm was written when Nathan the prophet came to David after he had gone in with Bathsheba and had murdered a man, Uriah, the Hittite. David was the God-selected king of the land, a man who willfully committed a sinful act. He had done the deed and he had committed the act. But, everything changed when he repented. The whole situation changed when he came to the Lord and asked for mercy, forgiveness, and cleansing.

His life-changing prayer continued:

> *Wash me thoroughly [and repeatedly] from my iniquity and guilt and cleanse me and make me wholly pure from my sin. For I am conscious of my transgressions and I acknowledge them; my sin is ever before me.*
>
> Psalm 51:2-3 AMP

When I read this, the Lord had me take note of the word "conscious." David was conscious of his sin (it was on his conscience) and if he had not come to the Lord and asked Him for help, the devil would have kept bringing the memory of this transgression to his conscious mind over and over and over again, completely hindering God's plan for his life.

The devil plagues many of God's people with reminders of their past sins and graphic memories of their past hurts. If you are one of those people, you need to know how to deal with that memory. If you don't, the reminders and memories will return you spiritually to the place they originated and, like a skip on a record, a CD or a DVD, continuously repeat. It is much like being caught in an eddy on the river, you get nowhere and nowhere fast.

The Lord showed me that when you face guilt and bad memories from the past, iniquity is working. He wants you to immediately ask Him for help. He told me to deal with that bad memory as if it were an evil spirit. Do not give it any place to work. There's no need to let it fester and grow and make you miserable and unproductive. He wants to deliver you from it so you can get back to doing His will for your life.

He said to me, *"When you face a situation in front of you that reminds you of an unpleasant situation from behind you, realize this: the situation in front of you is not old it is new. Ask Me to take care of the memory (the iniquity) from behind you first, then face the situation in front of you."* The key we are discussing, the key He revealed to me, enables you to stop, erase, eradicate and completely eliminate the paralyzing grip of those old memories. They will stop haunting you. They will stop paralyzing you. They will not plague you anymore.

This is precisely and exactly what King David did. The next scriptures show it clearly.

Notice what happened when David prayed and asked for help. He wrote,

> *Hide Your face from my sins and blot out all my guilt and iniquities. Create in me a clean heart, O God, renew a right, persevering, and steadfast spirit within me.*
>
> Psalm 51:9-10 AMP

Have you ever felt guilty, ashamed, or condemned? Then you need to deal with the iniquity causing it. Why? For the same reason David needed to deal with his. He did it so he could step back into the place, back into the grace of the immeasurable gift that God had blessed him with when he was anointed by the prophet, Samuel. Only then could he serve the people in the way God intended. David stepped into it, and so must you.

In Psalm 51:14, David uses an interesting combination of words as he continues his prayer to God:

> *Deliver me from blood-guiltiness and death, O God, the God of my salvation, and my tongue shall sing aloud of Your righteousness (Your rightness and Your justice) (AMP).*

When you look up this verse in other translations, you'll see the word "blood guiltiness" is the term for murder. His second sin was murder. He by committing the sin of adultery committed the very same sin satan had. His sin was unjust gain, he took another man's wife. He, at a time when the bible says kings go out to war, stayed home. His inaction led him to the place where he would take something that did not belong to him. The resulting iniquity caused him, just like Adam's original sin caused Cain, to take another man's life.

Yes, the iniquity from his sin made him take another man's life. In truth, it caused him to shed innocent blood, to murder.

Satan has, for centuries, been minimizing this murder under the guise of adultery. It reminded me of how iniquity had been minimized under the guise of sin. When I saw this truth, it added more fuel to the fire for me to completely expose satan's operation so he can be completely dethroned in every area of our lives.

So, to reiterate, from the above mentioned revelation, David prayed and asked the Lord to forgive him for adultery and murder and cleanse him thoroughly and repeatedly from the resulting iniquity, from the effect of the sin.

He prayed this prayer, *Deliver me from blood-guiltiness and death, O God, the God of my salvation, and my tongue shall sing aloud of Your righteousness (Your rightness and Your justice) (AMP).*

Notice with me the amazing result of that prayer. Immediately after God dealt with the iniquity, joy came out of David's mouth. His tongue was no longer controlled by iniquity and hurts. The death sentence was removed. The prison sentence was eliminated. The Joy of the Lord then consumed him, and he was able to step back into his God-given role.

To illustrate this point further, in an earlier example of David's zeal for God, we find the young boy going out against the giant Goliath when older men refused the challenge. The reason these men could not go is evidenced by their mouth. They had experienced the presence of the Lord before and experienced when His presence had departed from Saul. They knew it very well. They could perceive the separation. Iniquity then became the driving force behind their mouth.

In contrast, young David, who had the experience of being chosen by God, when the prophet Samuel anointed him with the horn of anointing oil, on the day he was anointed, the power of the Holy Spirit came upon him. He knew, right then and there, the Lord was with him. The presence of the Holy Spirit with him equipped and enabled him to approach the king. When he did, he said, (paraphrased) "Let me at him!" The king said, "I don't think so." But, recognizing the presence of the Lord with him, the king consented, saying, "If you're going to do it, use my weapons and my armor." (In other words, said, "Use the golden calf I had made to fight this battle.") But David, remembering all the other feats God had enabled him to accomplish, said, "No! I know what God has done for me!"

David was a man who understood his covenant and knew the Lord was with him.

As Christians, the key the Lord revealed and we're talking about here is part of our covenant. It is yours and it is mine. But unless we appropriate it, we will not reap the benefit of it. So the boy, David, went out to meet the giant Goliath. David boldly decreed to Goliath, "This day you're going down, and your carcass is going to be fed to the birds of the air." That's exactly what happened. Why? Because the Lord was with him.

God directed David to go with what he knew when selecting his weapon. It was "tried and true" for David. God had enabled him to defend his father's sheep and kill all manner of beasts with a slingshot and a smooth stone, so he stayed with what he knew God had shown him, what he had proven, and he selected five smooth stones.

The Lord is so concerned with what's best for His children that He willingly provides divine direction for all of us—our part is to spend time with Him, to hear what He has to say, to listen to what He has to say and do what He has shown us to do.

I've noticed that some of His directions are so simple and easy. For instance, He often says to me *"Five smooth stones."* This means to me, *"Go with what I have already shown you. Walk in the revelation I have already given you."* That is good advice for all of us. Every time we do that, the Lord will continue giving us more and more revelation. If we don't, the door is opened up to satan, as we just saw in the book Hosea where those priests had rejected the revelation of God, sin, iniquity, and all forms of perversion entered right in. So I admonish you, in Jesus' name, to embrace the revelation that God gives you with all your heart and move forward with the Lord. He is moving forward and so must you.

David did. He heeded God's direction. He took aim, released one of the smooth stones from his slingshot, and nailed Goliath. The giant fell down flat. Then, David took the giant's own sword, (the Lord revealed to me iniquity is actually called the devil's sword), and he cut off Goliath's head.

Why did he cut off the head? Because that uncircumcised Philistine's mouth was located there and that's the very thing that was talking down to him and the rest of the Israeli army the whole time.

When iniquity is in operation, the devil uses the memories of past sins and hurts against us to thwart God's plan for our lives. Those memories talk to us. Thoughts like: "Ever since that person did this or that to me ..." "Ever since this situation happened this is how my life's been ..." "Here we go again ..." "Not that, not again ..." "Ever since that happened this is the way I've been dealing with life ..." "You know, because of what I have done, because of how I messed up, I'll never amount to anything ..." "Why don't you just quit and give up ..." "You are such a failure ..." "I am going to be disappointed with you ..." "Why don't you just end it all right here ...?" "You know you can't fix all this so why don't you just take your life and end it all right here?"

The negative memories and suggestions that come like this are part of satan's weapons and arsenal against you and are used to hinder you, delay you, and to try to stop the flow of God's power in your life.

The Lord had given David awareness of this revelation, so he used the enemy's sword to cut off his head. He dismembered the giant and that uncircumcised Philistine stopped talking to him that very moment. That problem would never talk to him again.

Also notice this, as soon as that feat was accomplished, David was immediately catapulted into the plan God had for his life.

And do you know what else will happen? When you appropriate this promise in your own life, the Lord will do the same for you. He will stop the action of the enemy's plan against you and activate His plan for your life.

CHAPTER NINE

New Testament Scriptures about The Iniquity/Mouth Connection

After this, I asked the Lord to direct me to some more New Testament scriptures about iniquity. The first place He led me to was 1 John 1:9. He admonished me to look at it from this new, fresh perspective.

To make sure I was getting accurate information that conveyed the original meaning, I studied from Young's Literal Translation and Young's Analytical Concordance. If anyone understands anything about the original language, the man who wrote these books does. God gifted him to do this important work and he thoroughly studied it out. The Lord revealed to me this important piece of information: The King James Bible was translated at a time in history when Hebrew and Greek were not spoken languages. So some of the original purpose, intent and meaning were not part of the translation process.

First John 1:9 in *Young's Literal Translation* says:

If we may confess our sins, steadfast He is, and righteous, that He may forgive us the sins and may cleanse us from every unrighteousness.

In the first part of this verse it uses the word "may" which indicates a choice. Nothing God does for us is against our will. From the beginning days of creation when Adam was formed from the dust of the ground and the Lord breathed life into him, God has given mankind, the only part of creation made in His image and likeness, a free will.

We can choose to do this or we can choose not to. In other words, the two promises in the part of the verse that follows are conditional on us making the decision to do what is mentioned in the first part of the verse.

In the last part of this verse, the word "unrighteousness" is not the word "sin." It is the very same word the Lord brought to my attention earlier, the word "iniquity."

So let's read it again, this time substituting iniquity in the place of unrighteousness.

> *If we may confess our sins, steadfast He is, and righteous, that He may forgive us the sins and may cleanse us from every iniquity.*

He said He would forgive us of sin and He said He would cleanse us of every iniquity. Every emotional hurt, sense of shame, embarrassment, guilt, condemnation, all the emotional turmoil, every injury satan ever was ever able to do to us in our soul!

A lot of people who have equated iniquity/unrighteousness and sin will say, "But, Doc, God has already forgiven me of my sins."

That's right. That's true. That's great. You have been forgiven. God has forgiven you. I have been forgiven. That's where I was stopped, too.

But what I did not realize was this: I was walking around, with something in my soul, from every sin, transgression and hurt, right on my person, iniquity. Iniquity had separated me to such a degree from God's presence and had such a stranglehold on me I nearly was evicted from my body by a massive heart attack.

Jeremiah 17 explains this truth this way (paraphrased):

Our sins are written with a pen of iron with a point of a diamond. They are graven on the horns of the altar and also on the tablet of our heart.

Forgiveness absolutely removes the engraving written on God's altar, but unknown to you, you still carry the carbon copy of the engraving, the graven mark on the table of your inner most parts.

Iniquity is spiritual contraband. It hinders your prayers, separates you from God, disqualifies you from the plan of God, affects you to the point that it causes your mouth to spill out poison and makes you murder people with your words. It will also turn away God's intended blessings for your life and prevent your ministry offerings and the seeds you sow from being accepted by God.

Yes, you heard it right. Iniquity will mark every seed you sow for destruction and turn away the very harvests God has sent to bless you.

To prove this, the Lord led me to Jeremiah 5:25 KJV:

Your iniquities have turned away these things, and your sins have withholden good things from you.

Do you see it?

Sin withholds God's blessings, but iniquity turns them away.

Then read this in Psalm 51:19:

> *Then shalt thou be pleased with the sacrifices of righteousness, with burnt offering and whole burnt offering: then shall they offer bullocks upon thine altar."*

"Then" signifies "after." God will be pleased with your ministry offerings after the iniquity has been dealt with, not before.

So, iniquity, when it is present, has the hidden power to allow satan access to you and to control and manipulate your entire life.

At this point, the Lord reminded me of James 3:6-8. With this leading I discovered another vital answer to a previous question I had until He answered it in this study.

Speaking of the tongue, James, inspired by the Holy Spirit, said, *no man can tame it.* I had heard many explanations of this verse, all of which entailed using discipline and fleshly effort to control the tongue, but none satisfied my heart or produced any tangible results in my life. There were absolutely no results or good fruit from all the fleshly efforts to control the tongue until the Lord revealed this key about iniquity to me. This is the very reason why so many have such difficulty in controlling the tongue, which is often an offending member. Our Father God made a way for us to tame it, but we haven't known, until now, how to access it, so we have been perishing for lack of knowledge.

The Lord said to me, *"Read the whole verse again."* I did and it says:

> *And the tongue is a fire, a world of INIQUITY: so is the tongue among our members, that it defileth the whole body, and setteth on fire the course of nature; and it is set on fire of hell. For every kind of beasts, and of birds, and of serpents, and of things in the sea, is tamed, and hath been tamed of mankind: But the tongue can no man tame; it is an unruly evil, full of deadly poison. (KJV)*

I mentioned earlier that the Lord led me to Hebrews 9 and 10. They speak of the sacrifices of bulls and goats. In the yearly sacrifice was a yearly remembrance of sin. A plowing up of iniquity re-injured their souls and caused a perpetual stirring up, aggravation and irritation from their all their past problems. This annual sacrifice kept bringing up their past sins, mistakes and failures and kept driving their mouths. They kept re-visiting the same old problems. The same issues kept re-surfacing in their lives. They could not get free. They were trapped and locked in that prison. No amount of dotting all the "i's" or crossing all the "t's" or making big sacrifices and offerings or doing good deeds or doing good works succeeded in setting them free from the prison in which they found themselves. They were hopelessly and completely bound.

Joshua and Caleb, on the other hand, the only two out of these two million who were able to go into the Promised Land, must have had insight into the revelation God had given David, since they (with God's help) were able to harness their tongue and succeeded in making it successfully into the Promised Land.

The appropriation of this fresh, but original revelation from God activates the only thing that will tame the tongue. It activates the God-given power to control your tongue. It enables you to change the course of your entire life. It allows you to get your whole life, yes, your entire life, moving in the right direction again.

CHAPTER TEN

Results of Getting Rid of Iniquity

At this point, the desire to live free of the effects of iniquity overwhelmed me.

To fuel and feed the fire even more, the Lord then asked me, *"Would you like to know what will happen in your life after you get rid of the iniquity?"*

The family was all still sleeping and I did not want to wake them. So I shouted it out (with every fiber of my being) as loud as I could on the inside of me, "Yes, yes, yes!"

Are you ready for some more shouting material?

Job 5:15-16 AMP tells us this,

> *... [God] saves [the fatherless] from the sword of their mouth, and the needy from the hand of the mighty.*

This scripture says our Father God saves the fatherless (those who are not in, don't know about, or fully understand their covenant) from the sword of their mouth, (a sword, the devil's sword, was actually in their mouth) and the needy (again, those who are not in, don't know or understand their covenant) from the hand of the mighty.

This is exactly what happened when David cut off the head of that giant.

And look at the result. Job 5:16 AMP:

So the poor have hope, and iniquity shuts her mouth.

Wow! Iniquity shuts her mouth. Iniquity stops talking to you. Those issues stop speaking to you. They stop living in your present. They are shut up. Yes, yes yes!

God saved them from the sword of their mouth when they asked Him to deal with the iniquity. Destruction stopped working in their lives immediately.

But, in order for this to happen, in order for iniquity to shut her mouth, in order for all those issues to stop talking to you, the Lord told me it can only be done by the application of this key He revealed to me. He told me and I am telling you there is absolutely no other way.

This revelation is also the key to being able to do what is found in Job 5:22:

At destruction and famine you shall laugh, neither shall you be afraid of the living creatures of the earth.

Once the iniquity is dealt with, God empowers you to be able to laugh in the face of destruction without any fear and enables you to overcome in any situation.

This is good news. Do you want some more good news? More shouting material?

In this next scripture, after iniquity is dealt with, the Lord says:

> *And their sins and iniquities will I remember no more.*
> Hebrews 10:17 KJV

Our Father God says He will not remember your sins and iniquities anymore. He will never bring them up again. And not just the sin, but also the iniquity. He will not bring up what the sin did to you.

- He's not going to rub it in
- He won't add insult to your injury
- He won't make you re-live your past
- He won't pick off the scab
- He won't re-hash it with you
- He won't drag you back through the mud
- He won't make you re-visit the painful events in your life

He's not ever going to make you feel bad, guilty, ashamed, or embarrassed for anything you may have done. He will not injure or harm you while He is helping you.

What a loving, kind, merciful, graceful, and forgiving Father God.

You may not have been able to trust your earthly mother or father. You may not have been able to trust your brother or sister or your aunt or uncle or your grandfather or grandmother. You may not be able to fully trust your doctor, your lawyer or even your best friend, spouse, rabbi or pastor, but You can trust your Father God.

I asked the Lord how He was able to do this. How could He choose (He said "will I" so it was His choice) to not remember our sins and iniquities, and do you know what He told me?

He said, *"I am able to make the choice not to remember them using the very same key I am revealing to you right now. You will understand it fully when I show you the key."*

He then told me, *"I have a design, a plan for everything. All things are upheld by the word of My power."*

He then led me to Psalm 1:1-3. It says this…

> *Blessed is the man who walks not in the counsel of the ungodly, Nor stands in the path of sinners, nor sits in the seat of the scornful; but his delight is in the law of the Lord, and in His law he meditates day and night. He shall be like a tree planted by the rivers of water, that brings forth its fruit in its season, whose leaf also shall not wither; and whatever he does shall prosper.*
>
> Psalm 1:1-3 NKJV

In verse 3 it says something that, when He revealed it to me, was and is absolutely wonderful and liberating. It says, *everything he does prospers.*

Now I ask you, because the Lord asked me the very same question. Does everything include mistakes?

It does. If you are seeking the Lord for His way, with His heart, the grace of God will meet your every need. He will even give you the grace to overcome mistakes.

This truth alone will eliminate the fear of stepping out and doing what God asks you to do. He has provided the grace for it. The primary attribute He's looking for is willingness, and He has also provided the grace to enable you to be willing through the appropriation of this key He revealed to me.

Side note: At this point I feel I need to clarify something. I am not talking about giving someone a license to sin or permission to purposefully and willfully sin. People doing this are absolutely setting themselves up for the judgment of almighty God and need our prayers. Crying out for the mercy of God, repentance and remission of sin is the only answer for that situation. What I am talking about is making a mistake while you are walking out the plan of God for your life. A sin is a sin and a mistake is a mistake. A mistake is not a sin, and there has never been a baby born who was a mistake.

A perfect example was with Abram and Sarai. In the natural, they could not conceive a child, but they thought about the promise God told them for years. They both came to this conclusion: They thought maybe what God meant is that the child will come through their household, through Hagar, to accomplish the above mentioned goal. Out of that decision came Ishmael. Ishmael was not the child God had promised would come from Abram and Sarai, but He was not the mistake. Their decision to act without God was. The bible says that out of Ishmael God would make a great nation.

You may have come into this world differently than what someone may call a "perfect family." You may have been born into an awful situation, an unfortunate, nasty situation, out of wedlock or have been told you were a mistake. You are not a mistake. The Lord clearly showed me this is an absolute lie from the pit of hell, designed by satan, to keep you in bondage. The truth is this: Every person born is first a spirit, then given a soul, and lastly, a physical body formed by God within their mother's womb. The Lord then told me this truth, and with it came further revelation. He said this, *"When I want to change the world, I send a baby. So, tell my people this truth. Tell them I sent them, tell them I sent them on purpose, and tell them I sent them with My solution into the situation they found themselves in to bring My glory into the situation and to bring My resolution to the situation. Tell them I sent them to help Me fulfill My plan."*

With that in mind, in regard to His plan for your life and the grace to overcome mistakes, the Lord told me the primary characteristic He needs are willing vessels—equipped individuals who will allow Him to use them for His purposes. With this additional piece of information in place, He then revealed to me this next truth: He does all the equipping as we continue to appropriate this revelation in our lives.

Our part is to choose to participate, and God will enable us to do the rest.

If that is not enough encouraging news, look at more results of removing iniquity and setting it right in Job 11.

He said, *"If only you would prepare your heart and lift up your hands to him in prayer. Get rid of your sins and leave all iniquity behind you."*

Now, most of us have asked for forgiveness of our sin, but what is involved in leaving all iniquity behind us? How do we do that? The only way is by appropriating this covenant key the Lord showed me. In preparing to do God's will, the Lord showed me we must ask Him to do this for us, and He will do it.

Here is the result:

> *"Then your face will brighten in innocence. You will be strong and free of fear. You will forget your misery. It will all be gone like water under the bridge. Your life will be brighter than the noonday. Any darkness will be as bright as morning. You will have courage because you will have hope. You will be protected and will rest in safety. You will lie down unafraid, and many will look to you for help."*
>
> Job 11:13-20 NLT

This is a win-win situation.

What do we need in a time like this? With wars, rumors of wars and turmoil all around us? We need to be able to be steadfast and unafraid, because God is faithful, and He has a good plan for our lives. He said He has a plan for us that will give us hope and a future. He said that if we will apply this covenant provision, He would prepare us to do what He has called us to do.

Let's back up a few verses in that same passage in the New King James Version. He said, *you would forget your misery and remember it as waters that have passed away. Your life*, (your whole life), *will be brighter than noonday. Though you were dark, you would be like the morning. And you would be secure, because there's hope, yes, you would dig around you and take your rest in safety. You would also lie down and no one could make you afraid.*

Are you in a situation or have you ever faced a situation that made you afraid? God has a place of safety, a place of protection where you will have perfect peace. Appropriating this covenant promise positions you right in the middle of His place of protection.

Now why is all this so important? It's important because God has a specific plan for each one of your lives. The place He has for you is like Goshen. It is a place where you feel safe, a place of full provision and a place where you will seek and find His presence. It is a place where you will be enabled to overcome in every situation of life and you will become of great service in the Kingdom of God.

With that in mind, now look at Isaiah 41:8-13 in the Message translation. This is the result of what happens in your life when you appropriate this promise, when you honor the Lord and allow Him, as I did, to do this for you.

> *"But you, Israel, are my servant. You're Jacob, my first choice, descendants of my good friend Abraham. I pulled you in from all over the world, called you in from every dark corner of the earth, telling you, 'You're my servant, serving on my side. I've picked you. I haven't dropped you.' Don't panic. I'm with you. There's no need to fear for I'm your God. I'll give you strength. I'll help you. I'll hold you steady; keep a firm grip on you.*
>
> *Count on it: Everyone who had it in for you will end up out in the cold—real losers. Those who worked against you will end up empty-handed—nothing to show for their lives. When you go out looking for your old adversaries you won't find them—Not a trace of your old enemies, not even a memory. That's right. Because I, your GOD, have a firm grip on you and I'm not letting go. I'm telling you, 'Don't panic. I'm right here to help you.'*
>
> Isaiah 41:8-13 *THE MESSAGE*

God's words *"You, Israel, are my servant,"* include everyone who God has chosen to be part of His plan. What does that do for your faith? It makes mine skyrocket. When you have settled that in your heart and mind, you have put yourself in a place—as Jesus did—that makes you fit for the Master's use. You are prepared by God to function, just like Jesus did.

In John 14:30, it gives an example of how Jesus functioned. Again, from Young's Literal Translation, Jesus says, *"I will no more talk much with you, for the ruler of this world doth come, and in me he hath nothing."*

I had heard many people say that iniquity was mine, but that's not so—iniquity is something the devil brought to me.

Can you see that? Jesus said, *"...in me, he—the ruler of this world —has nothing."*

Do you know why Shadrach, Meshach, and Abednego couldn't be burned? Because when satan came on the scene, he found nothing in them.

John 14:30 in the Amplified Bible says it this way:

> *I will not talk with you much more, for the prince (evil genius, ruler) of the world is coming. And he has no claim on Me. [He has nothing in common with Me; there is nothing in Me that belongs to him, and he has no power over Me.]*

Now, consider Shadrach, Meshach, and Abednego in the fire now from a different perspective. In Daniel 3:24-25, King Nebuchadnezzar spoke to his counselors:

"Then why do I see four men walking around in the fire?" he asked. "They are not tied up, and they show no sign of being hurt—and the fourth one looks like an angel."

Notice, they were not tied up. Did you know that iniquity ties you up and makes you completely unavailable for the plan of God? Notice also, they showed no signs of being hurt.

To be used and useful in the Kingdom, you cannot afford to be tied up or hurt.

I submit to you, the reason they were able to go into that situation and come out not even smelling like smoke is they had no iniquity in them. They were not marked for destruction and disqualification from God's plan. Nothing of satan was found in them. In short, nothing was able to separate them from God's presence.

I also submit to you it is the reason the apostle John could not be boiled in oil and the apostle Paul could stand up in front of everyone of his day (after he had been used to persecute, jail, and terrorize Christians) and say he had harmed no man.

Paul was the man the Lord originally gave the revelation through to share with believers everywhere.

Under inspiration of the Holy Spirit, Paul wrote from a Philippian jail what is found in chapter 3, verses 13-15:

Brethren, I count not myself to have apprehended: but <u>this</u> one thing <u>I do</u>, forgetting those things which are behind, and reaching forth unto those things which are before, I press toward the mark for the prize of the *high calling of God in Christ Jesus. Let us therefore, as many as be perfect, be thus minded: and if in any thing ye be otherwise minded, God shall reveal even this unto you. (KJV)*

In the verses above, the underlined words were added by the translators as well as the punctuation. So this verse actually reads in its original context like this:

Brethren, I count not myself to have apprehended but one thing, forgetting those things which are behind ...

He was saying here that there were many things he had not yet apprehended, but the one thing he had apprehended was the revelation of how to forget.

Forgetting is also accomplished by the appropriation of this key the Lord revealed to me.

CHAPTER ELEVEN

The Key to Appropriate This Covenant Promise

At this point, I was really chomping at the bit. There was a real urgency in the symptoms I was dealing with. The chokehold was very strong, my breathing was labored, my left arm and jaw were numb, my heartbeat was fluttering and skipping and I felt like an elephant was on my chest. I was also struggling with these thoughts: How do I make sure Dr. Mary and all our boys are taken care of? What about them? How will they make it?

But, above all these thoughts, there was a greater authority and urgency in the sound of the voice of the Lord's leading. He kept urging me on.

The Lord then led me to Hebrews 9, for he had shown me the connection earlier with the word "conscience" in Psalm 51.

> *But [that appointed time came] when Christ (the Messiah) appeared as a High Priest of the better things that have come and are to come. [Then] through the greater and more perfect tabernacle not made with [human] hands, that is, not a part of this material*

> *creation, He went once for all into the [Holy of] Holies [of heaven], not by virtue of the blood of goats and calves [by which to make reconciliation between God and man], but His own blood, having found and secured a complete redemption (an everlasting release for us). For if [the mere] sprinkling of unholy and defiled persons with blood of goats and bulls and with the ashes of a burnt heifer is sufficient for the purification of the body,*
>
> *How much more surely shall the blood of Christ, Who by virtue of [His] eternal Spirit [His own preexistent divine personality] has offered Himself as an unblemished sacrifice to God, purge our conscience from dead works and lifeless observances to serve the [ever] living God?*
>
> Hebrews 9:11-14 AMP

He said the blood of Christ would, by the virtue of His eternal Spirit, purge our conscience from all the things that ministered death to us in our past.

Your conscience includes: memories, guilt, shame, hurts, condemnation, mental awareness, right versus wrong, good versus bad, this is where the record is kept, all the emotional turmoil, all of which are the building blocks and components of iniquity.

Then the Lord again said, "*When you face something in front of you that reminds you of something negative from behind you, ask Me to deal with the old memory before facing the new challenge.*"

The Lord asked me, "Is it really the same old problem?"

He then reminded me of another scripture. It says *when the devil is cast out he goes through dry places seeking rest finding none. So he returns not just by himself, but with seven other evil spirits worse than it.*

So the Lord said to me, *"You need to face this new challenge in a new way without any iniquity from your past."*

Not only that, but if you have anything on your conscience, you can pray but the Father's voice is not clear because your conscience has been marred by iniquity.

Now, let's get back to Hebrews 9:14.

This is the definition of the word *purge* used in Hebrews 9:14.

> 1a: to clear of guilt b: to free from moral or ceremonial defilement

After looking up this definition, the Lord reminded me, *"satan's constant occupation is trying to neutralize the power of the church and make it his own."*

When I read the term "ceremonial defilement," the Lord immediately reminded me of another term "religious tradition." Religious tradition can and will defile you. It is one of the few subjects mentioned in the entire Bible that completely shuts off and negates the power of God in every situation you find yourself in.

The Lord then took me to the book of Acts17 as there was a reference to the term "religious" in this passage.

> *So Paul, standing in the center of the Areopagus [Mars Hill meeting place], said: Men of Athens, I perceive in*

> *every way [on every hand and with every turn I make] that you are most religious or very reverent to demons.*
> Acts 17:22 AMP

He made this comment to these religious rulers in response to their inscription on their altar in their temple that said these words, *"To the Unknown God."*

I remember shaking my head. I said, "Lord, I do not want anything to do with being religious or reverencing demons."

I also remembered what the Lord had revealed earlier regarding His position on the condition of the churches satan had deceived and taken control over. "*You* (first My priests and then, as a result, My people) *refuse to recognize the revelation of God. It's the men who pick up the whores that I'm after. When they (the people) decide to get their lives together and go off looking for God once again, they'll find it's too late. I, God, will be long gone. You (priests) have played your sex-and-religion games long enough."*

Substituting this truth with this idea, we see this revelation: "*You have played your sex-and-being very reverent to demons games long enough."*

He then said to me, "*When you appropriate this covenant promise and ask me to do this for you, I will be removing the effect of every hurt, every bit of unrighteousness, all shame and condemnation, all the effects of all forms of moral and religious defilement and influences related to demon reverence and worship (the sex-and-being very reverent to demons games being perpetuated by the deceived priests) so you can serve Me in My kingdom."*

The word "purge" also denotes a deluge: the Holy Spirit, by the cleansing action of the blood of Jesus, lifts the standard against the enemy like the flood of Noah.

The Lord also had me look at these other two words: lifeless observances.

"Lifeless" denoting anything dead, and "observances" denoting anything I have observed.

He said, *"I will be purging your consciousness of the memories of anything and everything you observed in your life that ministered death to you in any form, spirit, soul or body."*

As I thought about this, the Lord said to me,

"I made provision for this in My sacrifice. I was wounded for your transgressions, and I was bruised for your iniquities."

He asked me, "What's a bruise to you, Doc?"

I said, "A bruise is the result of trauma to the soft tissues. In a bruise, the blood vessels have been broken and the blood is poured out."

And what does it (the poured out blood) do? The blood seeks and searches out every little hurt in the surrounding tissue and makes it whole again.

So, not only was He wounded for our transgressions, but He was also bruised for our iniquities. Both actions are different and both are important.

The scripture in Isaiah 53 went on to say, *"it pleased the Lord to bruise Him and he has laid on Him the iniquity of us all."*

I asked the Lord why he was pleased with this, as this was his only begotten Son. The Lord then reminded me of a medical truth. Every human baby carries the blood of the father. Jesus was no different. He was a vessel carrying the Father's blood.

The blood He carried enabled Him to do the plan God had for Him, and since that blood has been poured out on the mercy seat, it (and it alone) will enable us to do the same when we appropriate this covenant promise.

He then said, *"If you'll just ask me, I can completely remove all the iniquity and heal all those sins, transgressions and hurts and prepare you to fulfill My plan for your life. I'll even enable you and help you get willing."* I said, "Really?" And He directed me to Hebrews13.

We saw earlier that Hebrews 9 said the blood will purify or purge your conscience from dead works and lifeless observances so you can serve the living God, which is wonderful, but Hebrews 13 says something that is very interesting.

> *Now may the God of peace who brought up our Lord Jesus from the dead, that great Shepherd of the sheep, through the blood of the everlasting covenant, make you complete in every good work to do His will, working in you what is well pleasing in His sight, through Jesus Christ.*
>
> Hebrews 13:20-21 NKJV

You can see right here that He enables you to be willing. You choose to participate, then he does the equipping. The Lord said it to me this way, *"I do not call those who are qualified; I qualify those who I call."*

Now, let's read it from the Amplified Bible.

> *Now may the God of peace [Who is the Author and the Giver of peace], Who brought again from among the dead our Lord Jesus, that great Shepherd of the sheep, by the blood [that sealed, ratified] the everlasting agreement (covenant, testament), strengthen (complete, perfect) and make you what you ought to be and equip you with everything good that you may carry out His will; [while He Himself] works in you and accomplishes that which is pleasing in His sight, through Jesus Christ.*
>
> Hebrews 13:20-21 AMP

He said He would, by the blood of Jesus, strengthen you, complete you, perfect you, make you what you ought to be and equip you with everything good that you may carry out His will.

What an awesome deal. He not only said, by the key of the blood of Jesus, He would take away all the negative effects of sin and iniquity, but would also equip us to be used in the Kingdom.

After seeing this key, I said to the Lord, "According to what You have shown me, I can, just like David, approach you and ask you to do this for me over everything negative from my past and I can, just like Moses, intercede and stand in the gap for others and ask You to do this for them."

CHAPTER TWELVE

Appropriate the Covenant Promise: Get Prepared

The Lord then said to me *"Yes, you can. I have made the Way for you to be able do so."*

At this very moment, I decided to step across the line and fully trust the Lord regarding the situation I was in. He told me He would and I decided to believe Him. The symptoms were still there, but no longer did they have any of my full attention. It was like they were happening to someone else. I was able to see what was going on but was not moved by the situation. I just knew I had a part to play in the situation and knew it was time for my part.

Some of you may ask, "Wasn't that hard? How could you do that? How could you disregard and lay aside all your sound medical training and stand with what you believe the Lord told you?"

I'm glad you asked.

In July of 2010, months before this life-changing, God-touching experience, I had an open vision while driving to work. That particular day I was listening to a message in our vehicle. For the entire year before this point, the Lord asked me to listen to that particular message every day. In the middle of the message, inspired by the Holy Spirit, these words came across the preacher's lips: *"God's challenge from the beginning has been to get His people to believe that He said what He said, that He meant what He said and that He will do what He said He will do."* Immediately, I was in the Spirit. I saw an open field in front of me, completely plowed with dark black dirt as far as they eye could see with mountains in the background. Then, I saw a single, solitary dried out stalk. In the vision I could tell it was from a sunflower. The stalk was cut at a forty-five degree angle downward from right to left and I could see down into the hollow of the stalk.

I then saw the Lord's hand come in, remove that stalk with its tiny dried-up root system and toss it out of my field of vision to my right.

Next, in the place where the sunflower was removed, I saw the Lord place what looked like a sequoia. In a single movement He dropped it. I heard and felt a deep resonant sound. Shooom! He dropped it right into its place, along with its entire root structure intact.

You may say, "But what does that have to do with anything?"

What the Lord showed me is this: I had begun reading and studying in the Word, and every time I did, I was hiding it in my heart. It first began when I was very little. I found a small Bible in my great-grandmother's home and read the first chapter of John and the book of Revelation. The most memorable thing I remember was the adventure story. The Lord also showed me the field in my vision with the rich, plowed, black soil was my heart. It had been tilled and prepared. He showed me, just like the field I saw; every person's heart has different places for different things. Just like in a garden there is a spot for carrots, a spot for beans, a spot for corn, with a place and a purpose for every spot. The spot where the sunflower had been planted was the specific spot that had, in God's plan, been reserved for something else. This spot was the place in my heart where the seed of the foundational truth that God is faithful and true was supposed to be planted. But something else had gotten into its spot. As a result, before this point, I could not fully trust God. The things I had done in my life, I "just did them myself" (and in so doing, learned by experience). Looking back, I can see how God was helping me, but what I did not know during these years was this: My ability to trust Him was being hindered by a tiny sunflower that occupied that spot in my heart. A spot that was made for the faithfulness of my Father God.

Now you may ask, "Where did the sunflower come from? What prevented you from trusting God fully before this point?"

The Lord revealed to me this truth: *"The seed that produced the sunflower was planted when your mother and father separated and your father left you with your mother's family when you were four years old. Because they did not stay together, you believed I was unfaithful. The seed that got planted took My place in your heart and prevented you from believing Me fully."*

I grew up in my mom's and grandparent's (my mom's parent's) homes. I am so grateful to God He provided mother and father figures in my life. Some of the most important lessons I learned that helped me grow up quickly I learned through their lives. I saw living breathing examples right in front of me. I saw the importance of God through the lives of my grandparents and others God used. In their example, I witnessed how reliability, dependability and a good work ethic were important character traits to help prepare me for the calling of God on my life.

Later in life, after the birth of our first son, I began to seek for solutions and answers to the challenges I faced in raising a son diagnosed with cerebral palsy. The medical community had no answers, so I sought for help through what turned out to be just dead, dry religion. As I began to hear, experience, and listen to the voice of religion and religious works, I found it progressively more impossible to believe God for myself. I tried to listen for God's voice through other ministers and through their stories, but I found no success in operating the way they said God dealt with them. I had great success when I did things from my heart, like my grandparents did, before I got involved in the world of religion, but after getting involved in religion, with all the religious laws and thinking, the word of God I knew in my heart got choked out and everything stopped working. The more I worked at keeping all the "religious" laws, by doing all the "religious" things, the worse it got. Then, the Lord revealed to me this truth from the scripture, one in Romans 4, and another in Galatians 3, another in Ephesians 2, one from Philippians 3, and another from Hebrews 7. I am sure there are others as well, but these will suffice to bring across the point the Lord was revealing to me.

In Romans it says this:

"Clearly, God's promise to give the whole earth to Abraham and his descendants was based not on his

obedience to God's law, but on a right relationship with God that comes by faith. If God's promise is only for those who obey the law, then faith is not necessary and the promise is pointless. For the law always brings punishment on those who try to obey it. (The only way to avoid breaking the law is to have no law to break.)"

Romans 4:13-15 NLT

Then in Galatians:

"So all who put their faith in Christ share the same blessing Abraham received because of his faith. But those who depend on the law to make them right with God are under his curse, for the Scriptures say, "Cursed is everyone who does not observe and obey all the commands that are written in God's Book of the Law."

Galatians 3:9, 10 NLT

Then in Ephesians:

"Because by grace you have salvation through faith; and that not of yourselves: it is given by God: Not by works, so that no man may take glory to himself. For by His act we were given existence in Christ Jesus to do those good works which God before made ready for us so that we might do them."

Then in Philippians:

"But those things which were profit to me, I gave up for Christ. Yes truly, and I am ready to give up all things for the knowledge of Christ Jesus my Lord, which is more than all: for whom I have undergone the loss of all things, and to me they are less than nothing, so that I may have Christ as my reward, and be seen

in him, not having my righteousness which is of the law, but that which is through faith in Christ, the righteousness which is of God by faith:"

And lastly in Hebrews 7:11-12 and 18-19:

11 Now if perfection (a perfect fellowship between God and the worshiper) had been attainable by the Levitical priesthood—for under it the people were given the Law—why was it further necessary that there should arise another and different kind of Priest, one after the order of Melchizedek, rather than one appointed after the order and rank of Aaron?

12 For when there is a change in the priesthood, there is of necessity an alteration of the law [concerning the priesthood] as well.

18 So a previous physical regulation and command is cancelled because of its weakness and ineffectiveness and uselessness—

19 For the Law never made anything perfect—but instead a better hope is introduced through which we [now] come close to God. (AMP)

After He revealed this truth, I realized I had allowed myself to get shifted by satan (and a bunch of his Pharisees and Sadducees) into trying to be flawless and perfect. I was trying to live a perfect life, trying to do everything perfectly and flawlessly so God would heal my son. I was trying to do everything perfect so God would bless me, save me, heal me, deliver me, prosper me, and I was always coming up short. I kept failing repeatedly and had lost my way in the process.

The Lord then told me this staggering truth.

> *"I told you, My church, to make disciples, but satan deceived you and got you all twisted up. Instead you are making pharisees and sadducees.*

At this very moment, I realized I had let religion and religious works (demon worship) take a major stronghold in my life. Religious works had become god to me and made the Word of God (the things I knew God told me) no effect. Religious training and traditions had replaced God in my life. Just like the golden calf. Just like Aaron, when Moses was led up the mountain to actually meet with God, Aaron went into the tent. He stayed in the tent and then came out and said, paraphrased, "I have heard from god. Give me your gold. I need to make a calf, so you can see and worship god, the god who delivered you out of Egypt."

Aaron did not hear from God. If he had heard from God, he would have been praying, interceding, and comforting the people entrusted to him. Actually filling in for Moses while he went up the mountain, since the people were unable and did not believe they could actually hear from God, they got lead into deception. At this point in his ministry, Aaron missed God, but was later restored to his position in God's kingdom by activating this covenant promise.

I realized I was in that exact place. I had been deceived by satan, his messengers, and I was trapped in what I found out was nothing more than Baal worship.

This thought dawned on me, I am saved (this word encompasses every blessing in our Christian walk) by the blood of Jesus. By grace and by grace alone. Not by any amount of my works.

I then realized my absolute need for all my faith to be in the sacrifice Jesus made for me alone and for none of it to be in my works. None of my faith is to be focused on the pastor, my wife, my friends, my favorite evangelist, none of it to be focused in me, none in building my faith enough or making right confessions or walking in love good enough. All of these things can be godly character traits, and are fruit of the Holy Spirit, but are only made perfect by our Father God. They are only made perfect by the sacrifice Jesus made. None of these works are the god that will save you, prosper you, bless you, deliver you or protect you.

Our Father God alone is our shield, our strength, our fortress, our deliverer, our shelter, our strong tower and our ever-present help in time of need. We are only made complete by Him by our faith in Him, not by any work we do. The moment we shift and put our faith in the work we are doing, faith in religion, faith in making right confessions, faith in the size of our offering, faith in our walking in love good enough or faith in calling those things which be not as though they were. If we let this happen, we have moved from faith in God (which comes from what He actually tells you to do Himself) and faith in His perfect sacrifice, literally, to Baal worship. We have essentially created a "sacred calf" and now we (unknowingly) standing in direct opposition to the Living God and are denying the power thereof.

So, you may ask, what about works? Doesn't the Bible say that *"faith without works is dead?"*

Yes it does. I also found out, in this process, that there are works for us to do, but they are not works of the flesh. They are the very same ones mentioned that Jesus did. He said *"I must work the works of Him who sent Me."*

So, to reiterate and clarify this point, my works, the works I am to do are not religious works, not participating in demon worship. The works I am to do are to hear from my Father and do those things He shows and leads me to do.

Now, let's get back to the vision of the sunflower stalk.

When the Lord stepped in and removed the sunflower stalk, in that moment, everything changed for me. At that point, that very point when the faithfulness of God was restored, the Lord cleared all this up for me. He restored His faithfulness in my heart. I have had no issues believing and trusting Him since then.

Because of this, it was easy to trust Him in the face of those alarming symptoms. Nothing else I was doing was working to help my son or my family, and the worst thing that could happen is that I would leave my body. I knew if I did, I was going to Heaven, so what did I have to fear?

The Lord then asked me this question: *"Will you honor me and allow me to do this for you and your family?"*

I said, "Sure."

He then said something precious to me: *"I have been waiting for you to ask."*

At this moment, the scripture in James 4 came to my mind. It says in the 2nd and 3rd verses that, *"ye have not, because ye ask not. Ye ask, and receive not, because ye ask amiss, that ye may consume it upon your lusts." (James 4:2, 3 KJV)*

You can see from this scripture this point very clearly, having comes as a result of asking, and receiving comes as a result of asking for the right reason.

In this second example, you will see another aspect regarding asking. By asking the Lord to do this, we are actually fulfilling an ancient prophecy given by God himself through the prophet Ezekiel.

> *"Thus saith the Lord God; In the day that I shall have cleansed you from all your iniquities I will also cause you to dwell in the cities, and the wastes shall be builded. And the desolate land shall be tilled, whereas it lay desolate in the sight of all that passed by. And they shall say, This land that was desolate is become like the garden of Eden; and the waste and desolate and ruined cities are become fenced, and are inhabited. Then the heathen that are left round about you shall know that I the Lord build the ruined places, and plant that that was desolate: I the Lord have spoken it, and I will do it. Thus saith the Lord God; I will yet for this be enquired of by the house of Israel, to do it for them; I will increase them with men like a flock. As the holy flock, as the flock of Jerusalem in her solemn feasts; so shall the waste cities be filled with flocks of men: and they shall know that I am the Lord."*
>
> Ezekiel 36:33-38 KJV

The underlined words bring out this truth. On the day the iniquities are cleansed, God's wholeness and restoration process begins in every area of one's life. But let's focus on the second part:

> *Thus saith the Lord God; I will yet for this be enquired of by the house of Israel, to do it for them.*
>
> Ezekiel 36:37 KJV

The Lord said, *I will yet* (a later, set-time) *for this* (the cleansing of all iniquities) *be enquired of* (asked) *by the house of Israel* (this includes all Jews, gentiles, all peoples engrafted into the body of Christ) *to do it for them.* The Lord said there is a set time for this to be asked of Him. For me, that time was January 5th, 2011.

In addition, it is also not just asking, it is asking for the right reason, it is asking for the purpose of serving in the Kingdom, to operate in the Great Awakening, the end-time revival. To, as the scripture brings out, bring the truth of *"This Gospel"* to all people, to open their eyes to know the truth so that *"they shall know that He is the Lord."*

Through the application of the blood of Jesus, to pardon and cleanse every iniquity from our lives, our Father God will enable us to be dwelling, re-building, tilling, planting, fencing, inhabiting and re-creating His original plan for the earth which He began in the Garden of Eden.

So, you can now see, from the description of this prophecy, God's promise is mentioned there, but it must be appropriated. The Lord wants us to ask Him to do this, not only for us, but also for the entire body of Christ.

We are actually fulfilling this ancient prophecy when we ask Him to do this, and are activating the necessary key to the fulfillment of dry bones and the flesh becoming one new man as mentioned in Ezekiel 37 and the making of one new man from the two mentioned in Ephesians 2.

Then, in order to give me even more confidence in my asking, the Lord revealed to me this truth: Both of the scriptures He led me to in Hebrews 9:14 and Hebrews 13:20-21 have the right reasons in them. The reason being to serve in the Kingdom, to serve the ever living God, while He works in us that which is well pleasing in His sight, so

I knew that I knew, beyond the shadow of a doubt, He would honor them completely and fully.

He wanted me to come boldly into His very presence, right up to His throne of Grace to obtain this specific mercy and grace, right in my time of need, so I would be made able and qualified to serve in His Kingdom and be used to Him in helping fulfill His plan.

Inspired by the Holy Spirit, I then said to myself, "I am going to pray and ask You, Father, to do this for me and my family."

As a side note: I just wanted to let you know, just before I actually prayed these prayers, I was actually thinking these thoughts.

"If this is really true, if You are real, then You'll have to prove it to me, God."

I was in a place (because of past experiences of witnessing hundreds of religious unanswered prayers) that I was not even sure of the reality of what He had shown me. And the reality of the situation was I truly needed to see some genuine action, not just dead, dry words I had listened to in church for years.

Right then, I decided to pray these prayers. (Again, what did I really have to lose?)

I found out the answer to this question over the next days, months and years since I first prayed these prayers ... And so I give you these words of wisdom so you can be better prepared for what is to follow ...

You are initiating the purifying process put in place by our Almighty Father God!

You can read more about it in Hebrews chapter 10 and 12!

This promise and these prayers God has given us are paid for; He paid the price for them, but to follow through with Him will cost you everything... I encourage you as we and many others have, to let everything in your life be judged now and not wait till the day of judgement... For then it will be way too late!

It (God's purifying and refining process) is hand tailored for you. To say the least, it is very revealing! In the process, you may feel like you are being broken apart, unstitched, cleaned up, re-conditioned, stretched and restitched... Just know this: It is all for your good and necessary for your use in God's plan. You are being prepared for His new wine! (He can't put the new wine in the old skin!)

In the process, among other things, the Holy Spirit will teach you about Himself, His plan and show you His heart in the process! He will develop His fruits in your life! Remember, you are being equipped by the Precious Blood of the Lamb!

In this process, He will turn the hearts of the fathers to the children and children to the fathers, and He'll be showing you what really is important in your lives!

*As a side-note: Not everyone who is with you right now is supposed to go with you as you go through these "Gethsemene" moments with the Lord... Don't be concerned about that... They have not been selected by the Lord to go through what you go through... Not everyone will understand what you are doing or where you are going... Just keep your eyes in the Lord! Just as an olive press brings out the gift inside the olive, these times of pressing will be used by the Lord to bring out of you (just like the olive) the gift(s) He placed in you! And you will get more instruction about your part of His cross!

We all have one, you know!

This purifying process is initiated and directed by the Holy Spirit... He knows the correct timing for everything and just what you need to experience to accomplish the finished result: A warrior trained and prepared for use in His kingdom!

What you are going to experience is not a work of the flesh and cannot be drummed up. Only He knows what He made you and knows how to get you ready!

You are literally being called into service, His service! You will be given your marching orders to serve His purpose... No-one else has your part of His cross to bear... He will reveal to you and make you into the part you are supposed to be!

Remember, many are called, but few are chosen... When the Lord chooses you, go with Him!

In addition, I feel the Lord directing me to tell you this... As you go through the process, it is very good idea to have other believers (who the Lord will join you up with) and who have been brought through themselves and are filled with the Holy Spirit to encourage you as you go through the Holy Fire of God! You may feel fragile and undone, yet the Lord will use their encouraging words and witness to bring you peace, comfort and support.

The Bible makes it clear we are in a war, and so just know this... You are being prepared for war! You will have new growth in every area and also areas that need to be pruned, shaped and burned or removed...Keep moving forward!!!

God said in His word He is closing behind you a door no man can open and opening up before you a door no man can shut, so, literally, put the Blood of Jesus between your past and your present and let the Blood of Jesus move and propel you forward with Him!

And as I stated before, don't be concerned about being flawless and perfect...Just move forward with all your heart and stay teachable and pliable!

Having already begun this wonderful process myself, I encourage you to wholeheartedly pray these prayers, for yourself, from your heart and authorize God to initiate the process and to move on your behalf.

He will prove Himself faithful and true to you. He will bring you all the way through to victory.

These are the prayers I actually prayed.

"Father God, I am coming to You in Jesus' Name. I repent. I repent from trying to deal with this iniquity myself. I am done with trying to live my life and make decisions without You. I repent for allowing religion or any of my works to become a god and take Your place in my life. I repent from doing anything motivated by money and I repent for unknowingly worshiping demons. I am asking You, according to the multitude of Your tender mercies to perform Hebrews 9:14 for me and my family. I am asking you, by the blood of Jesus, to pardon every iniquity, to purge and purify my conscience from every iniquity. I am also asking you to purge my consciousness from every dead work and every lifeless observance that satan and every one of his messengers ever brought to me through sin, transgression, or hurt. I am asking you to fully pardon me. Subdue every iniquity, remove the punishment, destroy the power and consequence of every sin, transgression and hurt, and make me wholly pure from them by the blood of Jesus so that I can serve You, my Father, the ever-living God."

"In addition, I am asking you to perform Hebrews 13:20-21 for me. I am asking You, by the blood of Jesus, to strengthen me, complete me, perfect me, make me what I ought to be and equip me with everything good that I may carry out Your will, while You Yourself work in me and accomplish that which is pleasing in Your sight. I am asking to do this in Jesus' name and I am asking You to seal this prayer with the blood of Jesus. Amen."

Suddenly, in the twinkling of an eye, I felt the death grip on my body leave.

All the heart-attack symptoms were gone. Sitting there on that couch, with my family sleeping comfortably in their beds, immediately, I could actually breathe better than I could ever remember. Everything smelled fresh and clear. I was free. Undeniably free. Unquestionably free. In just a single moment, in what I found turned out to be the presence of the Lord, I was at complete peace. I was happy again. I was full of Joy! I was rejoicing! I was filled with laughter!

The Lord then spoke to me these words: *"I had it planned for you all along. It was all part of my plan for you to actually meet ME, the joy of your salvation. I have wanted you, for many years, to not just believe I could do this for you; I have wanted you to actually experience the reality of what I have done for you. Your hope was deferred and deferred and deferred and it made your heart sick. It is through the exceeding greatness of My Love for you that I desire you to experience the tangible reality of My kept promises in your life. A promise kept is far, far greater than a promise never kept. It would be absolute hypocrisy for you and your children to just hear about My promises or to hear Me make a promise without My ever really causing it to come to pass in your lives."*

I said, "Really. I thought I was just to believe no matter what."

And he finished it with this: *"The experience you just had is available for every one of my children. It is my desire that every one of my children not just believe, but actually experience Me. I want them to experience My glory, intimacy and presence, even while they are still on earth. They do not have to wait until they die and go to heaven to enjoy the manifestation of My presence or My promises in their lives. Tell them they can spend time with Me, their Father, their Heavenly Father right here and now. Tell them they can actually experience (in their own lives) all that I promised for them right here and right now."*

He then took me back to Acts 17.

> *The God Who produced and formed the world and all things in it, being Lord of heaven and earth, does not dwell in handmade shrines. Neither is He served by human hands, as though He lacked anything, for it is He Himself Who gives life and breath and all things to all [people]. And He made from one [common origin, one source, one blood] all nations of men to settle on the face of the earth, having definitely determined [their] allotted periods of time and the*

> *fixed boundaries of their habitation (their settlements, lands, and abodes), So that they should seek God, in the hope that they might feel after Him and find Him, although He is not far from each one of us. For in Him we live and move and have our being.*
>
> Acts 17:24-28 AMP

He made the way into His presence so we could seek Him, in the hope that we might feel after him and find Him. That word "feel" means to handle, to touch, to hold, to manipulate (as a baby who is standing on your lap will grab a hold of your nose, your cheeks or your hair or your ears). It means to experience. He wants all of us not just to believe in His promises or just to believe in Him, but to experience Him, His very presence, so we will not just believe, but know, by experience for ourselves, the love of Christ. He wants us to intimately know Him and not just believe, but be fully aware, tangibly aware (with our senses) He is with us everywhere we go.

I said that to Him, "Wow! That's awesome. That's wonderful. You are wonderful. Thank You for saving my life. Thank you for giving me my life back. Thank You for manifesting Yourself to me. Thank You, Thank You, Thank You, Lord."

He said this to me again, *"I had been waiting for you to ask."*

CHAPTER THIRTEEN

FILLED WITH ALL THE FULLNESS OF GOD

As I sat there, enjoying His Holy presence, enjoying the tangible manifest presence of God in my home, the Fire of God, breathing absolutely normal, feeling completely free in my body, the Lord said, *"Remember the four words I gave you related to this revelation? Forgiven, Pardoned, Prepared and Filled?"*

I said, "Yes."

He then said, *"Now you have been prepared to be filled with My glory."*

He explained further, *"My Word is alive and powerful, sharper than any two-edged sword, able to cut to the very division of soul and spirit, the joints and the marrow."*

He then asked me a question. *"As a doctor, what is the relationship between the joints and marrow?"*

I said, "The marrow is contained within the joint structure."

The Lord then said, *"Such it is with the soul and spirit. The spirit is contained within the vessel of the soul."*

He then reminded me of the story of the potter in Jeremiah 18:3:

> *And the vessel that he made of clay was marred in the hand of the potter; so he made it again into another vessel, as it seemed good to the potter to make.*

The Lord said to me, *"satan's plan was to mar your vessel, to crack your vessel and make it unfit for My use. In so doing, when one of my children receive of My precious Holy Spirit, their marred and cracked vessel cannot hold My glory, but rather, it runs through them like a tub with the stopper wide open."*

He also reminded me of my high school art class. In one of the semesters I took a pottery class. At the start of the class we went on a field trip to locate the clay. After finding the clay, we dug it out of the spot where we found it and took it back with us to the room where the potter's wheels were located. We then wet the clay repeatedly, worked with the clay till it was soft and pliable with all the lumps and bumps removed, mounted the clay on the wheel, and began working the clay. After several failed attempts and different experiences involved with learning how the process worked, we made our vessels on the wheel, shaped them, trimmed them, smoothed them and finished them. After this, we put them in the drying closet to allow them to dry very slowly so they would not crack. We finished the entire process by glazing them, kiln drying them until they began to sing from the fire's heat and then, lastly, testing them.

The test of our pots was three-fold.

The first test was visual. The pots were inspected. They were many different shapes and sizes and each one responded differently when the heat of the kiln was applied. We also got to see the effect of the glazing process. Glaze when it is applied goes on clear, but changes and reacts when the heat is put to it, so it is very interesting to discover what colors and patterns resulted from the glaze reacting with the heat. Every piece of pottery is absolutely individual and unique.

The second test came with the application a small hammer. With the hammer would tap the side of the pot and listen to the sound that came out of that pot. Good pots would sing a clear note when struck on their side. But the marred and cracked pots (the ones that did not stand the test of the fire) once struck would make a very dull sound. "NNRRRNT." It sounds very much like grumbling, complaining, and gnashing of teeth.

The third test was to fill the pot to the brim with water. The good pot would hold the water and be able to transfer it from one location to another. The hardened, marred and cracked pots would not hold the water, but allowed the water to run right out through the cracks in the pot down the side of the pot, onto the table and spill on the floor.

Side note: The above mentioned hardened and cracked pots were not very useful in their current condition. They were thrown into another pile in the room, a pile that was later taken and broken down into very small particles like sand and remixed with new clay in order to make new vessels. God, in His infinite wisdom, can even used old, hardened, cracked and rejected pots. All they had to do was to submit to the process of Him remaking them into another vessel. So if you are one of those hardened pots that is currently not of much use, just submit yourself to the Lord and say, "Here am I, Lord, use me." The Lord will break down all the hard parts and remake your vessel into a vessel of honor.

The Lord then told me this, *"By asking Me to purge all the iniquity from your life, you positioned yourself to be able to tap into My reservoir for the outpouring of the Holy Spirit in your life. By appropriating My promise to prepare you by the Blood of Jesus, I took all the pieces and re-made your broken, cracked vessel into a new vessel, a vessel of silver containing apples of gold. I then glazed and sealed you by the Blood of Jesus. I gave you My Joy. I put My song in your mouth and I enabled you to carry the precious treasures of My Holy Spirit so you can distribute them to those in need."*

He then reminded me of Luke 11:9-13.

> *And I say unto you, Ask, and it shall be given you; seek, and ye shall find; knock, and it shall be opened unto you. For every one that asketh receiveth; and he that seeketh findeth; and to him that knocketh it shall be opened. If a son shall ask bread of any of you that is a father, will he give him a stone? or if he ask a fish, will he for a fish give him a serpent? Or if he shall ask an egg, will he offer him a scorpion? If ye then, being evil, know how to give good gifts unto your children: how much more shall your heavenly Father give the Holy Spirit to them that ask him?*

He said He would give us the gift of the Holy Spirit if we would ask.

Then, in Ephesians 3 it says:

> *God's desire is to "grant you out of the rich treasury of His glory to be strengthened and reinforced with mighty power in the inner man by the [Holy] Spirit*

> *[Himself indwelling your innermost being and personality]. May Christ through your faith [actually] dwell (settle down, abide, make His permanent home) in your hearts. May you be rooted deep in love and founded securely on love, that you may have the power and be strong to apprehend and grasp with all the saints [God's devoted people, the experience of that love] what is the breadth and length and height and depth [of it]; [That you may really come] to know [practically, through experience for yourselves] the love of Christ, which far surpasses mere knowledge [without experience]; that you may be filled [through all your being] unto all the fullness of God [may have the richest measure of the divine Presence, and become a body wholly filled and flooded with God Himself]."*
>
> Ephesians 3:16-19 AMP

He said His desire is to give you this experience. He wants to fill you with all His fullness, not just you making noise with your mouth! He is not interested in making you look like or sound like a fool rattling off nonsense out of your mouth... In fact, He told me this truth: *"They (the church) have jumped over Me to tongues! The tongues that sat on them on the day of Pentecost and the tongues they spoke in are not the same tongues!* While it is definitely possible for you to speak in an unknown language (tongue) when the Holy Spirit comes upon you, is just as equally possible for you, just as countless others have, to speak the Word of the Lord with boldness or to prophesy, to see a heavenly vision or have a divine encounter with Him... It's time to take God out of the box and let God be God! What I will say to you about my experience with Him is this: When you ask Him to do this, He will fill you with the richest measure of His divine presence, with the fullness of the Godhead when you ask Him to do this for you.

With all these things in mind, I then said, Lord, I want you to do this for me.

I prayed this, and I wholeheartedly encourage you to do the same: "Heavenly Father, I am asking You to perform Luke 11:13 for me. I am asking You, by the blood of Jesus, to baptize me with the fire of the Holy Spirit, and fill me with Your precious Holy Spirit. I am asking you to fill my vessel to overflowing so I may share Your glory and share Your goodness with those I meet. I am asking to do this in Jesus' name, Amen."

As I prayed this, I felt a very strong wave of the power of God come over my body from head to toe. He baptized me with the fire of the Holy Spirit and filled me to overflowing with His precious Holy Spirit. I was filled with power from on High. I felt what seemed to be a fire start, right down in my belly.

Then, in light of this, He had me look at 1 Corinthians 2:12.

> *Now we have not received the spirit [that belongs to] the world, but the [Holy] Spirit Who is from God, [given to us] that we might realize and comprehend and appreciate the gifts [of divine favor and blessing so freely and lavishly] bestowed on us by God. (AMP)*

The Lord did this so we, by the Holy Spirit, will realize and comprehend and appreciate. So we will know and tangibly experience the gifts He bestowed on us.

He said further, *"Now, practice Ephesians 5:18 and you will continue to receive all the gifts of the Holy Spirit I have prepared for you. Then, carry these treasures and distribute them to everyone I lead you to. You are fit for My use and prepared for My plan."*

Ephesians 5:18 says this:

> *Don't be drunk with wine, because that will ruin your life. Instead, be filled with the Holy Spirit, singing psalms and hymns and spiritual songs among yourselves, and making music to the Lord in your hearts. And give thanks for everything to God the Father in the name of our Lord Jesus Christ.*
>
> Ephesians 5:18-20 NLT

CHAPTER FOURTEEN

The Second Vision: Iniquity and the Return of Jesus

Five to six months later, in August of 2011, the year in which the Lord completely delivered my life from certain death, began the process of cleansing me from every iniquity, prepared me by His blood and filled me with His Spirit, I had a second vision related to iniquity: this one was from a completely different perspective from the first vision.

I saw myself as a passenger flying in an airplane, looking out of a window on the left side of the plane. I knew I was sitting in a seat in front of the wing because there were no obstructions in my vision. At first, above, I saw the bright, clear, blue open skies with the sun shining brightly (an open heaven) but then, below, I saw a thick blanket of clouds. In the beginning parts of the vision, I could not see through the clouds at all, but as we continued on our trip, the blanket of clouds began to dissipate in certain areas. Every place where the cloud cover had dissipated, I could see all the way through to the ground and I could see the brilliant shaft of sunlight shine through and touch the ground.

As the Lord began to reveal to me this perspective, I saw something else I had never considered, but had always wondered how it happened.

The Lord reminded me of His departure and of His coming. At His departure, He ascended up, out of sight until He was completely beyond view. Why did he go? He had finished His race. What compelled Him to go? The blood He carried was all poured out. It was no longer enabling Him to stay. Quickly, the presence of iniquity on the earth repelled him like reversing a magnet. It did so to the point it completely separated Him, physically, from the earth below. Now, as the day of His return approaches, the separation is being removed. Heaven is coming to earth. At every place where this truth is applied and the iniquity is pardoned, purged and purified, an opening in the thick blanket of separation is created. A portal allowing full and complete access to the third Heaven opens up and the atmosphere of Heaven above is able to again touch the earth. He gave us the ability, by His own blood, to remove the mark satan put on our individual lives, families, neighborhoods, counties, states and nations and bring Heaven to earth in true manifestation in every one of our lives. He is also, by His own blood, setting the stage for His coming, preparing us, by the precious blood of the Lamb of God, without spot or wrinkle, to participate in His plan, the Great Wedding Feast and spend all eternity operating in His kingdom with Him.

The Lord then said to me, *"These things I am revealing to you are especially important as you see the day of My Son's return approaching."*

This next scripture, (Matthew 24:4-14, KJV), helps illuminate this very clearly.

4 Jesus answered and said unto them, Take heed that no man deceive you.

5 For many shall come in my name, saying, I am Christ; and shall deceive many.

6 And ye shall hear of wars and rumors of wars: see that ye be not troubled: for all these things must come to pass, but the end is not yet.

7 For nation shall rise against nation, and kingdom against kingdom: and there shall be famines, and pestilences, and earthquakes, in divers places.

8 All these are the beginning of sorrows.

9 Then shall they deliver you up to be afflicted, and shall kill you: and ye shall be hated of all nations for my name's sake.

10 And then shall many be offended, and shall betray one another, and shall hate one another.

11 And many false prophets shall rise, and shall deceive many.

12 And because INIQUITY shall abound, the love of many shall wax cold.

13 But he that shall endure unto the end, the same shall be saved.

14 And THIS gospel of the kingdom shall be preached in all the world for a witness unto all nations; and then shall the end come.

Let's look again at verse Matthew 24:12:

And because iniquity shall abound, the love of many shall wax cold.

The word love, here, is agape, the God kind of love, the love of God. And iniquity, when it is present will completely repel and choke the love of God out of your life. (And since God *is* love, it will literally choke Him out of your life).

Spiritually, through the working of iniquity, satan has been successfully separating people from the presence of their Father God and forcing them to function like it was before the veil was torn in the temple, forcing them to operate under a Baal system of worshiping mammon, getting bound in sexual perversion, killing God's prophets and doing everything in his power to hinder and delay the return of Jesus.

Satan has been trying to return us to a place like it was when there was very limited access to the presence of God and he had free reign in our lives.

In the Amplified translation of verse Matthew 24:12, is mentioned the phrase *"multiplied iniquity."* Sin is sin. Every sin or transgression carries a certain amount of iniquity and creates a certain amount of separation. Now multiply it and you can see how satan has been operating. Temptation, sin, and then separation. Injure, hurt, damage and then more separation. Multiply it a little more, a little more, a little more, and then attack like a lion when the person is very separated, right when they are vulnerable to be overtaken.

In 2 Thessalonians 2, we see another aspect of iniquity related to the coming of Jesus.

For the mystery of iniquity doth already work.
2 Thessalonians 2:7 KJV

This is one of the mysteries of the Kingdom. Satan knows and has known about this mystery and has been using it (often with a great degree of success) to operate against God's children from the beginning of time. But now, thank God, this mystery has been solved.

I submit to you this truth: To you pastors, leaders, moms and dads, grandmas and grandpas, aunts and uncles, as the Lord just revealed to us through these scriptures, one of the primary conditions of the people you are ministering to is not only one of being backslidden, but rather, they have been separated. They have been:

- Cut Off
- Injured
- Forsaken
- Lost
- Left behind
- Forgotten
- Left for dead
- Marked by iniquity
- Distanced from God through the mystery of iniquity and separation

Do you remember I mentioned earlier a connection between Jesus' coming and workers of iniquity? The Lord said to me, *"As you minister to other people, I encourage you to look at them the way I do—separated from Me by iniquity."*

He told me to tell you this:

There are literally millions and millions of people, who, just like I had done, call themselves christians, who do believe in me, have made a confession of faith and have devoted their lives to me and to service in My kingdom, but ...

They have literally never met Me!!! The iniquity from their sins, transgressions and hurts will keep them completely separated from My Presence!

Therefore, never minister to other people and do what you do for the motivation of financial gain or to obtain money! He also told me to tell you to refuse to minister condemnation or guilt. To back up what he said, He gave me this stern warning from Matthew 7:22-23 and Luke 13:26-28. Both of these passages mention very clearly Jesus' stand and position for all who work iniquity. He is not talking to sinners here, He is talking to ministers. disciples. People who have "committed their lives" to "serving His people." In both passages, He said these words:

> *"Depart from Me, all ye workers of iniquity. I never knew you."*

It is one thing for you to know about Him, but quite another for Him to know you ... I encourage you to submit your life to His inspection, His sanctification and His purification ... That way, you know-that-you-know, He knows you!

With this truth in mind, it is also vitally important as we see the end approaching that we, the children of the living God, make much of the blood of Jesus, remind ourselves about the power of the blood of Jesus and apply the blood to every sin, transgression or hurt.

To not do so is to commit perhaps the most serious sin of omission... Not teaching His people about appropriating the cleansing, redeeming, sanctifying, strengthening, equipping and restoring Blood of Jesus in their lives!!

It is imperative to teach those we minister to how to get rid of iniquity, live free from iniquity and prevent themselves from being separated from the presence of God by iniquity. Doing so will also prevent us from delaying or hindering His return [as He is returning for a church without spot, blemish, or wrinkle (all of which are descriptions of iniquity)]. As mentioned earlier, while writing about the definition of the word "iniquity," we found it includes the definition of a stamped impression. The word in the book of Revelation that is synonymous with this definition is the term "mark." I also submit to you this fact for consideration: The coincidence of these two terms and the similarity of their definitions leads me to believe that in a very tangible way, in a way we can truly grasp and understand, one of the major components of the "mark" of the beast is iniquity.

Through the continuous application of the blood of Jesus, our Father God keeps us free from the effects of all the enemy's devices. The blood of Jesus equips us and thus keeps us from receiving the mark of the beast and from being marked for destruction. It keeps us centered in the love of God. Our Father God said, *"in Him we live and move and have our being."* He has made the way, by His grace, supplied through the blood of Jesus, administered by the Holy Spirit, for us to live in love, stay in love, abide in love and dwell in love. All this so we can actually carry out His plan and will for our lives.

The application of this next verse of scripture will also help enable you to do this.

> *But you, dear friends, must build each other up in your most holy faith, pray in the power of the Holy Spirit, and await the mercy of our Lord Jesus Christ, who will bring you eternal life. In this way, you will keep yourselves safe in God's love.*
>
> Jude 1:20, 21 NLT

By believing in the blood, applying the blood and staying behind the blood, you are doing your part. As you wait on the Lord in His presence, you will receive the great exchange of your strength. He will exchange your strength. You will be filled with the Holy Spirit and He will keep you right at the center of His love.

IMPORTANT: If anything happens to you where you sin and miss it or if someone hurts you, (even if it is little or seems insignificant) immediately go to the Lord. He is your loving Father. Ask Him for forgiveness and forgive the offender, but then *remember to ask him to do the part only He can do.* Ask Him to pardon, cleanse, purge and purify you of every iniquity, of all unrighteousness, by the blood of Jesus so you can step right back into His plan. Ask Him to fill you with the precious Holy Spirit, to fill you with His treasures from heaven, step back into your place and finish your race with Joy.

An example here will bring you more light and allow you to see how it works in real life:

We have been blessed with four sons. Occasionally, something may happen where one of them (while playing with one of their brothers) gets hurt somehow. Here is a situation where we can apply this truth.

One brother hurt the other brother and one brother got hurt.

After the incident, the one who got hurt is crying and telling on the other. In addition, the one who caused the hurt is trying to shift the blame and explain what happened, both are doing so with very great emotion.

Then, they come to me or their mom, usually crying. They want to get our help.

We encourage them to "make it right with your brother." We have seen them apologize to each other and forgive each other and even hug each other very quickly and at first it looks like things are okay.

When we come back and check on them later, their mouths tell of their condition. If they did not get Father God involved, they continue whining and complaining and fussing about the new challenges they are facing.

It looked like they had made amends, but something is still not right. They had a form of godliness, but denied the power thereof. They did not get Our Father involved.

I ask them, "Did you make it right with your brother?" They answer, "Yes."

I then ask them "Did you ask Father God to do His part? They would answer, "No."

For the one who hurt the other, I then show him how to have Father God do His part; "Father God, I am asking you, by the blood of Jesus to forgive me, cleanse me and fill me with Your precious Holy Spirit."

For the one who got hurt, I then show him how to have Father God do His part;

"Father God, I am asking you, by the blood of Jesus to take away the hurt, cleanse me and fill me with Your precious Holy Spirit."

In so doing, the iniquity is removed and their fellowship is restored. And not just between the two of them but also with their Father God. They are immediately happy, joyful and smiling again. (And ready to help when we call on them to clean up their room.)

CHAPTER FIFTEEN

LET'S SUM IT ALL UP

The last couple places He led me in this study completely summarize the truth of the revelation He delivered to me.

The first place is in Ephesians 1:3-14 (*THE MESSAGE*):

How blessed is God. And what a blessing he is! He's the Father of our Master, Jesus Christ, and takes us to the high places of blessing in him. Long before he laid down earth's foundations, he had us in mind, had settled on us as the focus of his love, to be made whole and holy by his love. Long, long ago he decided to adopt us into his family through Jesus Christ. (What pleasure he took in planning this!) He wanted us to enter into the celebration of his lavish gift–giving by the hand of his beloved Son.

Because of the sacrifice of the Messiah, his blood poured out on the altar of the Cross, we're a free people—free of penalties and punishments chalked up by all our misdeeds. And not just barely free, either. Abundantly free! He thought of everything, provided for everything we could possibly need, letting us in on the plans he

> *took such delight in making. He set it all out before us in Christ, long–range plan in which everything would be brought together and summed up in him, everything in deepest heaven, everything on planet earth.*
>
> *It's in Christ that we find out who we are and what we are living for. Long before we first heard of Christ and got our hopes up, he had his eye on us, had designs on us for glorious living, part of the overall purpose he is working out in everything and everyone.*
>
> *It's in Christ that you, once you heard the truth and believed it (this Message of your salvation), found yourselves home free—signed, sealed, and delivered by the Holy Spirit. This SIGNET from God is the first installment on what's coming, a reminder that we'll get everything God has planned for us, a praising and glorious life!*

The word "signet" means "sign." The "sign" is what we experience when we ask the Lord to do this for us. We actually experience being engrafted into Him. We actually tangibly experience Him (the fire of God) and experience His love.

The second place He showed me is Hebrews 10:14 (*THE MESSAGE*):

> *It was a perfect sacrifice by a perfect person to perfect some very imperfect people. By that single offering, he did everything that needed to be done for everyone who takes part in the purifying process.*

Let's look at that last part of that last verse.

He did everything that needed to be done for everyone who takes part in the purifying process.

Let me ask you this, since He did everything that needed to be done, what is left for us to do?

Let me answer it quickly, just as the Lord answered me, none of the things He did in His perfect sacrifice.

Our job is to take part in the purifying process. Our job is to participate in His plan. Our job is to run the race that is set before us.

On a practical note, regarding my taking part in the purifying process, once the Lord cleansed me of the iniquity in my soul, He encouraged and instructed me to go through all my personal effects (photos, keepsakes, bookshelves, computer files, cabinets, clothes drawers, closets, file cabinets, drawers, possessions, storage places, sheds; in short, everywhere I kept stuff) and eliminate and eradicate anything in those locations that did not remind me of a bear or lion experience. The Lord reminded me of the story of David and Goliath: David said, when he was facing Goliath, *"I remember the lion and I remember the bear."*

The Lord told me to keep the things that reminded me of victories and accomplishments, and get rid of any and all of the things in those places that reminded me of anything from the past that had a negative memory or experience attached to it.

He said to me further, *"If you open a closet or a drawer and there are things in that drawer that take you back and remind you of negative experiences, you'll be giving satan a place; you'll be allowing him to keep opening up the wounds*

I healed you of and delivered you from again and again and again."

I actually enjoyed this part. The Bible clearly says this, "Be angry and sin not."

Instead of yielding to anger and flesh (and taking it out on those around me), I used the strength that came when I saw things in these places that reminded me of old bad memories to clean out all the old junk. This workout was liberating. Every time I went through the drawers and got rid of old stuff with old negative memories, the exercise of doing this brought more and more freedom and more and more liberty. It reminded me of the story of Naomi and Ruth in the Bible. Naomi's instructions to Ruth were for Ruth to get rid of the old garments, clean herself up, get some new garments and anoint herself. That way she would actually be available to do the next thing God had for her to do (in this case to be a wife to Boaz).

Now, my job every day, (the works I actually do every day) is to hear from God and do the things He leads me to do (and everything He leads me to do He will actually put on my heart to do). The Lord reveals to us in His Word that we will actually have the desire, the want-to, the ability to, the capability to do all He is asking us to do. He said, as we delight ourselves in Him, He will give us the desires of our heart. He will actually put His desires in our heart. And these will actually be desires that are holy, worthwhile, beneficial, and will fully meet the needs of the people we are ministering to. They will actually go home with the answer they were looking for. They will go home healed, delivered, saved, rescued, set free and equipped to do what God has made them to do.

Our works, then, the works we are to do, are just the same as Jesus did. He worked the works of him who sent Him. Our works are to "work the works of Him who sent us."

So, as we can see, there is a God-given plan to handle sin, forgiveness. There is also a God-given plan to handle iniquity, the footprint of sin. Iniquity must be cleansed by the blood of Jesus.

Both are important. Both are different. And both have to be appropriated.

They require our participation.

I encourage you to make the most of everything God has for you.

If you sin, take part in the process of forgiveness.

Then, take part in getting rid of the iniquity. Take part in the purifying process by way of the Blood of Jesus.

Side note: As you go through this process and past issues & circumstances come to your remembrance, remember this: You must keep moving forward with the Lord! When they come up (and they will), ask the Lord to wash you fresh and anew, much like a pot on the stove that has boiling water with chicken for dumplings in it; The scum and impurities in the chicken will come to the surface of the water as it boils and must be skimmed off repeatedly before the chicken is ready to be used in the recipe... So must the dross from our lives be cleansed thoroughly and repeatedly... Yes, contrary to many popular "teachings," I said thoroughly and repeatedly... Some situations you have been involved in can, if left untouched by the Holy Spirit, mark you for life! I mentioned king David's situation earlier. He had committed two sins, adultery and murder, both of which carried life sentences, and he knew he could never live out the sentences connected to them! I encourage you, just as David, I, and now thousands of others have, to let the Lord wash you fresh and anew REPEATEDLY of every iniquity by way of the the Blood of Jesus until you have no more consciousness... Until you literally have no more awareness whatsoever of those past sins, transgressions or hurts!

Allow your Father God to remove all the iniquity and let Him anoint you with His precious Holy Spirit and fire. He will enable you to put your past mistakes and failures behind you and actually live. In this way He will equip you to live your life to its fullest and you will actually accomplish all He created you to do.

CHAPTER SIXTEEN

Conclusion: The Spirit Without Measure

As you can see, God has a wonderful plan for your life. He wants to use you in His plan. He wants to use you to help fulfill His prophecy delivered by Isaiah and usher in the second coming of Jesus.

By appropriating the blood of Jesus and allowing our Father God to remove all the separation caused by iniquity and set things right, you have obtained access right into His very presence. He has enabled you, by the blood of Jesus, to live and dwell in a thin place, a place where there is no separation between Heaven and earth. In this position, you can, right where you live, by the grace of Almighty God, bring the Glory you received from being in His presence back to earth. He will also be preparing and positioning you right in the middle of His perfect plan so you can do His will for your life.

In this place, you can operate just like Jesus, with clean hands, just as it is written in Job 22:21-30 NKJV:

"Now acquaint yourself with Him, and be at peace;
Thereby good will come to you.

Receive, please, instruction from His mouth,
And lay up His words in your heart.
If you return to the Almighty, you will be built up;
You will remove INIQUITY far from your tents.
Then you will lay your gold in the dust,
And the gold of Ophir among the stones of the brooks.
Yes, the Almighty will be your gold
And your precious silver;
For then you will have your delight in the Almighty,
And lift up your face to God.
You will make your prayer to Him,
He will hear you,
And you will pay your vows.
You will also declare a thing,
And it will be established for you;
So light will shine on your ways.
When they cast you down, and you say, 'Exaltation will come!'
Then He will save the humble person.
He will even deliver one who is not innocent;
Yes, he will be delivered by the purity of your hands."

All the capabilities mentioned above become a tangible reality in your life when you do your part: By taking part, by participating in the purifying process, you are returning and acquainting yourself with Him, laying up His words in your heart, getting rid of iniquity and making the Almighty your precious gold and silver. Then, after the Lord has given you clean hands and a pure heart, you can pray (and be heard), you can make Godly vows and keep them, you can declare and decree His spoken will and it will truly come to pass, and you can actually be a genuine help those you come across who are in trouble.

When your hands are clean and your heart is pure, God will give you light into different situations you come across. From this place, instead of passing judgment, instead of being a judge, you can do something productive. You can actually intercede for someone you see in trouble (where judgment is due, where agreement is not being exercised, where the line of authority has been compromised, where words have been spoken against the resolution of the problem, where strife rules, where bewitching, voodoo and witchcraft are being exercised) and God will hear your prayer, respond to your prayer and deliver them. And to top it all off, God can use you in situations like these without any fleshly strife and without any contention.

From this place, God will send you forth, just like Jesus, into sticky, awful situations filled with anger, strife, contention, envy, jealousy and discontent in order to bring His righteousness, His peace, His joy and His solution to those in need. You will hear and speak the messages God gives you and do the deeds God shows you to do. When you hear from Him what to say and do what He shows you to do, He said He will give you, just as He did for Jesus, the Spirit without measure to meet the need of the situation.

> *For since He Whom God has sent speaks the words of God [proclaims God's own message], God does not give Him His Spirit sparingly or by measure, but boundless is the gift God makes of His Spirit! The Father loves the Son and has given (entrusted, committed) everything into His hand.*
>
> John 3:34, 35 AMP

Yes, this scripture was originally written about Jesus, but it also applies to any person in His body who will take part in the purification process and take the time, in His presence, to see and hear what He wants you to do. God will equip you, if you allow Him, to operate just like Jesus. Hearing from your Father, seeing what to do, and then acting out the instruction He gives you. You, by the grace of God, supplied by the blood of Jesus and administered by the Holy Spirit, become fully equipped. You can go, just like Moses did before Pharaoh. You can go right into a situation where normally death would be eminent, and come out shining with God's mission accomplished. All because you were fully equipped to do all God is calling you to do, without any fear and with complete confidence.

And, to reiterate, what will that accomplish? The will of God will be accomplished in the given situation. The person you are ministering to will be saved. They will be healed. They will be delivered. They will be set free. The situation will be solved and the Kingdom of God will be established. Right there in the middle of the sticky, awful situation. Right here on earth, just like it is in Heaven.

And to top it all off, you can do this as a brand new Christian, as a maturing believer or as a tried and tested warrior in the Kingdom. Every one of us can have full, complete, and undeniable access to the throne-room of heaven by the Blood of Jesus. You can, just like one of the very first people who came forward after our very first meeting where we shared this vital revelation, you can (just like she did) go from being unsaved, critical and judgmental to serving God in the Kingdom. And literally, you can do it in the twinkling of an eye. With just a touch from our Lord and Master, everything will begin to change. In just an instant, just a short period of time with Him, everything wrong can and will be made right so you can step into His plan and begin to make progress.

I know, just as I experienced for myself, at the moment you appropriate this word, His word, He will rescue you, bring restoration to you and transform your life.

Within days of the Lord revealing this truth to me, we began witnessing countless times, with our own eyes, Him actually open blind eyes, deaf ears, heal damaged and severed nerves, heal the lame, remove cancer and restore that which was medically incurable! We are daily witnessing Him, first hand, with our own eyes and ears, restore health and heal people (our son included) of their previously medically incurable wounds!

My heart's desire is for you to know Him and experience the power of His resurrection, find fellowship in His sufferings, in His life, and actually live the life He has for you to live. I want you to know how to put this revelation into practice, and how to appropriate it in your own life. I want you to discover your gifts, God's plan and actually fulfill His call on your life.

I know in my heart that the Lord has spoken specific things to you and has done Amazing things for you (and in you) that have prepared you for His plan.

Take the time to write us and let us know how His Word and this revelation have impacted your life.

Dr. Raymond P. Marshall

POSTSCRIPT

At the end of what was perhaps the very darkest hour of our family's life (two very distinct seven year periods in a row) much like an intense shaft of sunlight pierces through a thick veil of clouds on a very cloudy day, the Words of this song came out of my spirit.

I had never heard them sung this way before. "The Melody and rhythm was much like "The Night Before Christmas" mixed with "A Cat in the Hat!" The Lord and His angels sang them to me. As they did, there was a particular emphasis on the words "only" and "whiter," an emphasis that solidified this revelation as truly supernatural and completely took the natural and finite limits off of His infinite work.

Here they are:

Only the Blood

Chorus:
ONLY the Blood!
ONLY the Blood!
ONLY the Blood!
The Most Precious Blood!
ONLY the Blood!
ONLY the Blood!
ONLY the Blood!
Makes me Whiter than snow!

Verses:
Only the Blood!
Only the Blood!
Only the Blood!
Will remove iniquity!

The Blood strengthens me! And Perfects me!
The Blood Completes me! And Equips me!

Only the Blood!
Only the Blood!
Only the Blood brings me to stand in
Your Holy Presence!

Only the Blood!
Only the Blood!
Only the Blood!
Makes me able to do what You have called me to do!

Bridge:
Not how I call it,
Not what I say,
Not by my faith,
No other way...

Only by Way of the Most Precious Blood!!!

Not by my strength or the works that I do...
Not my perfection...
He cleared that up too!
Not by the quantity of the words that I say...
Only the Blood takes all the tears away!

Only the Blood puts the spring in my step
    and the song in my heart!
Only the Blood gives you a good place to start!

Coda/Ending:
So, if you are facing a problem much bigger than you,
Trust in the Blood, He'll make a Way through!

He'll lead you and guide you every step every day...
Trust in the Blood... He'll enable you to stand!

As you walk down this road and go His Way...
One thing is sure...
Only by the Blood can you fulfill His Plan!

And what about the critical, religious and proud?
The Lord said, "Forget them, they are a waterless cloud!"

The fake and the false need bodyguards at the meeting
And if you stay there with them, you'll be in for a beating!"

Adulterers and adulteresses will steal you blind...
So, take it from me, steer clear from their kind!"

So what is the MYSTERY? I'm glad that you asked!!!
ONLY the BLOOD Makes you fit for the task!!!

It will Strengthen, complete & perfect what you do...
You've heard all about it, now how about you?

It will make and equip you with everything good...
By now you know it's something you should!

So, take the time to Ask God and Pray...
Lord, will You wash all the INIQUITY away?
You'll be glad that you did...
I'm soooo excited!

When God finishes the work,
You'll awaken, morning by morning, having been knighted!!!

You'll be prepared for whatever comes your way...
Together with God you be able to say...

I'm ready, I'm ready, I'm finally ready!
And when you step out, He'll help keep you steady!

Your steps have been ordered, And you will finally see…
He's made the Way for you and for me!"

Dr Ray

From Jeremiah 29, Psalm 51, Hebrews 9 & Hebrews 13

POSTSCRIPT II
(P.P.S.)

AN ALL-IMPORTANT ADDENDUM...

Are You Prepared for the Days Ahead?

Just three days before Passover 2014, The Lord delivered to me the last eight pieces of the revelation you just finished reading regarding *The Truth About Iniquity.* My guess is He just didn't want them delivered until that very point. As it turned out, these final eight pieces were each extremely precious and, at the same time, very important. They were ALL VITAL pieces of the puzzle and needed to be included!

Fortunately, He also blessed me a very flexible publisher who was, to my amazement, miraculously able to take these final gems, incorporate them into the manuscript in the places where they belonged and bring them to life in the final printing. Way to go, SparkPubMedia!

After sending the final (I thought) e-mail attachment, I was resting and feeling good about completing the task at hand. I put the computer to sleep, took a shower and went to bed.

As I fell asleep, I was thinking about the details of the book, how everything miraculously came together and was thanking God for giving me the Grace to complete it.

Something else was on my mind, though. I was thinking about the upcoming Blood moon. It was to be the first of a cluster of four (a tetrad) and the last one had not occurred since 1967-68 (before I was born) so, as I fell asleep, I was very excited to have the opportunity to witness this historical event.

I was fully planning to get up and see it… But that is NOT what happened that night!

What happened was an unfolding I had not anticipated nor expected. That night, another connection was made, a VITAL TRUTH was shown and the next step of my next assignment was revealed! As I write these words on this page, it is with fear and trembling I emphatically express this truth to you: these words and the revelation you are about to read may be one of the most important messages you have ever read or seen. I feel like a watchman on the wall, and I just had something revealed to me. Something is headed this way that will change all of our lives FOREVER!

Here it is:

About midnight, in the middle of very sound sleep, I heard a sound go off inside of me. It sounded exactly like the shot of a gun! It immediately awoke me in my spirit… I was still fully and completely asleep physically, but, at the same time, I was fully aware of what had just happened. I knew I had heard this very sound before!

The first time I heard this sound, I was in junior high school. I was participating in a summer track program and had just been "promoted" to run the two mile race at the state meet in Charleston, West Virginia. But, you need to know this: my promotion did not come through my dazzling performance and record-setting winning of races. My promotion was due to the members of the senior team being disqualified from participating in the state meet. Somewhere along the way, they got way off-track and were got caught doing it. They were sidelined and the junior team was next in line.

I was very young, and at the time of the race was recovering from a terrible bicycle wreck. (I had scabs from head to toe on my whole left side, stitches in my upper lip, a broken collar bone and was still wearing a green sling on my left arm.) To top it all off, I was a sprinter! (Or so I thought). The longest distance I had ever run was 400 meters, but I was, to my surprise (both literally and figuratively), placed in the position of those who were previously qualified to run the race!

What a position I found myself in!

At the starting line, I saw there was a man with a hard plastic case in his hand. He was just standing there watching the events. At the appropriate time, however, he opened the case, took out a gun, loaded it and raised his arm in the air. All the runners in the race leaned forward a bit and so, inexperienced as I was, I just did the same.

When he pulled the trigger, the sound of that gun going off went through me in a way I will never forget. Even now, thirty one years later, I remember it vividly—I felt it with every fiber of my being as the sound entered my ears and then shot out the top of my head, the palms of my hands and the soles of my feet. I took off and ran like I never had before—I ran and ran and ran—I ran so hard I rolled across the finish line in fourth place in a race and a distance I had never run before!

With that in mind, let's get back to that soul-striking but very familiar sound from Passover 2104.

When I heard that very same sound go through me at midnight, IMMEDIATELY, I heard the Lord say,

"My son, it's the beginning of the race to the end."

He then reminded me of something else I had seen before. It just popped into my mind, right into my consciousness.

I remembered when I was a young boy, I had a green safe bank and the bank had a red combination lock with white numbers. The inner workings of the lock had three tumblers. You would turn it to the right to the first number, back to the left passing the second number once before you stop on the second number and then back to the right for the last number. With all the tumblers in proper alignment, the safe could be opened and the contents inside could be enjoyed.

However, at one point I forgot the combination to the safe. I had lost paper the numbers were written on and I could no longer open the safe. I did not give up on it, though. I worked with it and worked with it and eventually figured it out. Each time a tumbler fell into place there was a sound. I listened to the sounds as I moved the combination lock around. It was as if time stood still when the final tumbler fell into place and it opened!

The Lord then told me,

"You could only do it yourself because it had three. Everything you deal with on earth is in three dimensions. With the

additional tumbler, with four tumblers, and with the fourth dimension, it becomes infinitely harder. In fact, it's impossible for you to do it yourself without My help!"

His statement reminded me of the four Blood moons and how they, just like the tumblers in a safe, only manifest or occur when everything in the entire universe is in proper alignment. Then I remembered what was written in the old testament, where the prophets of old had described in visions given by the Lord seeing wheels within wheels and suddenly, everything came together, a glimpse into the Heavenly realm and His plan...

The wheels within the wheels, the tumblers, the safe, the sound...

Four Blood moons, four precise alignments, an opening into the fourth dimension and then as I mentioned in previous chapters of this book, the return of our Messiah, Jesus, our Lord and Savior and our safe passage through!

With that being said, in a way I may not seem to fully express, I need to tell you this: there is an urgency in this message like I never knew before and an extremely important piece of information you need to see, grasp and understand.

I know I may appear young and inexperienced and in many of your minds I may not appear to be what you think an elder should be... But, I did not pick me! I got picked!

The Lord showed me some things of vital importance to me and to you. I am just the delivery boy. After everything my family and I have been through, I told the Lord, "Just don't waste any of my pain! If what we went through can benefit someone else, please use our lives to help others make it through!"

The Lord gave me this vital piece of instruction regarding iniquity and I am passing it on to you. I encourage you to take it, apply it and then share it with everyone you know. Time is of the essence! Three of the four Blood moons have already passed.

The pearl from the scriptures the Lord gave me comes from Isaiah.

It says this in chapter 26,

20 Come, my people, enter your chambers and shut your doors behind you; hide yourselves for a little while until the [Lord's] wrath is past.

21 For behold, the Lord is coming out of His place [heaven] to punish the inhabitants of the earth for their iniquity; the earth also will disclose the blood shed upon her and will no longer cover her slain and conceal her guilt. (Isaiah 26:20-21 AMP)

When I read this scripture, knowing what The Lord had shown me about iniquity, I thought, "Lord, You just gave me the very answer Your people need to pass the final test before they enter the New Heaven to be with You! The presence (or absence) of iniquity will be the determining factor as to the direction a person goes after this life; To spend eternity with You or to spend eternity separated from You!" I then immediately remembered something I saw when I was a little boy. In my mind's eye I saw a block of cheese with a cheese slicer and the piece of cheese cut off and separated from the rest.

I then said within myself, "Iniquity is the cheese slicer!"

The Lord then said to me,

"Yes, son. You are correct. And I want you to know I made the process foolproof. Please, tell my people how I have everything perfectly arranged for each of them to be able fully pass the test. This place (earth) down where you live is broken and cannot be mended. It is past being repaired. This age is coming to a close and the only thing left to do is for Me to do My part, the part only I am qualified to do."

The Lord took me to Ezekiel 36. It says this in verses 22-38.

> *22-23 "Therefore, tell Israel, 'Message of God, the Master: I'm not doing this for you, Israel. I'm doing it for me, to save my character, my holy name, which you've blackened in every country where you've gone. I'm going to put my great and holy name on display, the name that has been ruined in so many countries, the name that you blackened wherever you went. Then the nations will realize who I really am, that I am God, when I show my holiness through you so that they can see it with their own eyes.*
>
> *24-28 "'For here's what I'm going to do: I'm going to take you out of these countries, gather you from all over, and bring you back to your own land. I'll pour pure water over you and scrub you clean. I'll give you a new heart, put a new spirit in you. I'll remove the stone heart from your body and replace it with a heart that's God-willed, not self-willed. I'll put my Spirit in you and make it possible for you to do what I tell you and live by my commands. You'll once again live in the land I gave your ancestors. You'll be my people! I'll be your God!*
>
> *29-30 "'I'll pull you out of that stinking pollution. I'll give personal orders to the wheat fields, telling them*

to grow bumper crops. I'll send no more famines. I'll make sure your fruit trees and field crops flourish. Other nations won't be able to hold you in contempt again because of famine.

31 "'And then you'll think back over your terrible lives—the evil, the shame—and be thoroughly disgusted with yourselves, realizing how badly you've lived—all those obscenities you've carried out.

32 "'I'm not doing this for you. Get this through your thick heads! Shame on you. What a mess you made of things, Israel!

33-36 "'Message of God, the Master: On the day I scrub you clean from all your filthy living, I'll also make your cities livable. The ruins will be rebuilt. The neglected land will be worked again, no longer overgrown with weeds and thistles, worthless in the eyes of passersby. People will exclaim, "Why, this weed patch has been turned into a Garden of Eden! And the ruined cities, smashed into oblivion, are now thriving!" The nations around you that are still in existence will realize that I, God, rebuild ruins and replant empty waste places. I, God, said so, and I'll do it.

37-38 "'Message of God, the Master: Yet again I'm going to do what Israel asks. I'll increase their population as with a flock of sheep. Like the milling flocks of sheep brought for sacrifices in Jerusalem during the appointed feasts, the ruined cities will be filled with flocks of people. And they'll realize that I am God.'" (Ez. 36-22-38, MSG)

As you can see from this scripture, the prophet Ezekiel was giving divine insight into a day much like the day we live in today. Today is absolutely impossible to even drive down a highway without your vehicle being covered by dirt and grime and specks of tar. It is impossible to go a day without needing a bath. Talk to any mom or dad with children and they will tell you that doing laundry and cleaning up messes are some of the most important and frequent tasks we have at hand. The atmosphere on earth is so polluted with iniquity, the only way we are able to live here is by the Grace of Almighty God!

The Lord also expanded the definition of iniquity for me since He first revealed the difference between iniquity and sin. He wants all of us to know the extent of what He showed me. The definition (that denotes the CHARACTER of sin and as such makes it completely different from sin) includes and is an integral part of:

- Earth's bloodstains
- Injury to the land
- The word "defilement"
- The wages of sin
- "Death" itself
- The sting of death
- The curse of the law
- The curse of the fall
- The punishment of sin
- The power of sin
- The mark of sin
- The stain of sin
- The mark of the beast
- The damage of sin
- The repercussion of sin
- The fallout of sin
- Stubbornness
- Idolatry

- The weight of sin
- The victory of the grave

This list is not all inclusive, but is simply an expansion of the original revelation to include anything and everything that is the result of sin, the result of transgressing God's Law, the result of grieving the Holy Spirit or the result of you causing injury to another person.

Every one of these (as well as any other source of iniquity) results in spiritual weight being added to your being. Sins, transgressions and hurts will lord themselves over you but the resulting iniquities will weigh you down. You do not need to be carrying any extra weight while you are running your race. It will take everything you have to finish your race, so I encourage you let Him do the job that only He can do: unload you of every iniquity so you can finish strong!

Hebrews chapter 12 says it this way,

> *1 Wherefore seeing we also are compassed about with so great a cloud of witnesses, let us lay aside every WEIGHT, and the SIN which doth so easily beset us, and let us run with patience the race that is set before us, 2 Looking unto Jesus the author and finisher of our faith; who for the joy that was set before him endured the cross, despising the shame, and is set down at the right hand of the throne of God… (Hebrews 12:1-2)*

As you can see, weight and sin are two separate items and each needs to be overcome. This passage goes on to talk about being disciplined for a long distance race.

The Lord also told me to tell you this: He knows the day and hour we live in, He knows the condition of the place where we are, He knows who are His and He's got us all covered! Yes, we each have our assignments to finish, and there are iniquities all around us, but, He is coming back to take us all home. So, all the more importantly, at this day and hour, we must do our part to stay focused, avoid distractions and we must be about our Father's business. I encourage each and every one of us, myself included, to do our creative best with what we have been given and run our race to the finish!

Yes, as you just read, you read it right! When the Lord returns for His people, there will be just one deciding factor, just one test to pass and just one scanner/detector to go through. It will be the Answer to the questions, "Have you been washed in the Blood? Are you still washed in the Blood? Is there any iniquity to be found?"

It will not be how perfect you are, how perfectly you perform, how many good works you do or how diligently you tithed. It will be simply be the answer to these questions: Did you bow your knee and give Him full access to your whole life? Does He have access to your heart and soul and did you allow Him to cleanse and keep you cleansed of every iniquity along the way?

He is doing one last housecleaning (a very thorough one at that) and He will not leave one stone unturned—there will be one final shaking. When He is finished, all the historic and religious junk will be revealed, exposed and removed so only the unshakable essentials are standing, clear and uncluttered.

To put it in real-world terms, we need all hands on deck! It's time for all you grandfathers, uncles, dads and brothers to get all the trash out and help the grandmothers, aunts, moms and sisters. It's time for all of us to get rid of worthless pursuits and pursue the plan of God. It's time for all the babies to have their faces wiped, diapers changed, teeth brushed and hair fixed and for everybody to quit messing around and get on the train.

I know this is strong, but it needs to be said! This is the most recent piece of the puzzle the Lord showed me regarding iniquity and with it, comes the only way for you, your family and all your loved ones to have unhindered access to that fourth dimension when our Lord returns. He said His coming would be AFTER you see all these signs (the Blood moons are in fact just the beginning of these events) happening all around you, so look up, your redemption is drawing very, very near!

After I saw what is coming and I saw what He showed me, I knew I had to tell you. The Lord wants you to have in your hand everything you need to be able to relax in your spirit so you can focus, meet and fulfill all the demands of the critical days ahead!

Side note: To all of you who have been going through an extremely hard and rough spot... In other words, you've really been going through it over the past few months or years, the Lord gave me this to share with you, from Isaiah Chapter 40:1-11 (AMP)

> 1 Comfort, comfort My people, says your God.
>
> 2 Speak tenderly to the heart of Jerusalem, and cry to her that her time of service *and* her warfare are ended, that [her punishment is accepted and] her iniquity is pardoned, that she has received [punishment] from the Lord's hand double for all her sins.
>
> 3 A voice of one who cries: Prepare in the wilderness the way of the Lord [clear away the obstacles];

make straight *and* smooth in the desert a highway for our God!

4 Every valley shall be lifted *and filled* up, and every mountain and hill shall be made low; and the crooked *and* uneven shall be made straight and level, and the rough places a plain.

5 And the glory (majesty and splendor) of the Lord shall be revealed, and all flesh shall see it together; for the mouth of the Lord has spoken it.

6 A voice says, Cry [prophesy]! And I said, What shall I cry? [The voice answered, Proclaim:] All flesh is as frail as grass, and all that makes it attractive [its kindness, its goodwill, its mercy from God, its glory and comeliness, however good] is transitory, like the flower of the field.

7 The grass withers, the flower fades, when the breath of the Lord blows upon it; surely [all] the people are like grass.

8 The [a]grass withers, the flower fades, but the word of our God will stand forever.

9 O you who bring good tidings to Zion, get up to the high mountain. O you who bring good tidings to Jerusalem, lift up your voice with strength, lift it up, be not afraid; say to the cities of Judah, Behold your God!

10 Behold, the Lord God will come with might, and His arm will rule for Him. Behold, His reward is with Him, and His recompense before Him.

11 He will feed His flock like a shepherd: He will gather the lambs in His arm, He will carry them in His bosom and will gently lead those that have their young.

So, as a servant of the Most High, I proclaim to you His message for this hour...

If you have been going through it, first and foremost, know this...

You are His!!! He's got you and will not let you go!!!

Also, The Lord wants you to know this...

The time your service *and* warfare are ended, [your punishment is accepted and] your iniquity is pardoned, that you have received [punishment] from His hand double for all your sins.

If you know of someone who has not been going through it, run the other direction. Do not worry or give a second thought about them. Run and don't look back!

Second, and of equal importance...

The Lord has heard your cries by reason of your taskmasters... You have had your arm twisted and were forced to do tasks that were not His bidding... He knows about it, is not at all happy about it and is coming to get you out of there! So, hang on and hold on, hang on and hold tight...

Help is on the Way!

The Lord may have been delayed and hindered in His getting to you, but He will be there to rescue you as fast as He can.

I don't know about you, but, just delivering this word from our Heavenly Father brings a smile to my face!

What this message from The Lord literally means is this:

In order for this word to be fulfilled, the manifestation of everything the Lord has shown you has finally come to pass!

Whoo-hoo! Yes! That's shouting material!

So, to wrap this all up, the train is in the station and the passengers are loading. Our Heavenly Father is waiting until the last of His get on board and is making sure our passage is secure.

I leave you with just a few questions: Are you on board? Is there anything preventing you?

You may have been forgiven for everything you have done, but have you asked our Father to remove and cleanse you of any iniquity?

If not, there is still time. We are somewhere past the middle of the race to the end.

I hope and pray I'll see you soon, on the other side!
Dr. Raymond Marshall

About the Author

Dr. Raymond P. Marshall is a devoted husband, father, doctor, gardener, author, pioneer, songwriter, inventor and fixer of broken things. Dr. Ray's life was changed after hearing what had happened to him as an infant: "After a traumatic birth, I was on a respirator and having seizures. My Uncle came to the hospital and made an alignment on my spine. After the intervention, I began to breathe on my own and stopped having seizures. Later, when I found out what had happened to me, I said, 'That's what I'm going to do!'"

Growing up in the hills of West Virginia in a very primitive home, all odds were against him. But destiny reigned, and after High School, he attended Marshall University, where he met his wife Dr. Mary Marshall. They were married in 1992 and attended Palmer College of Chiropractic where they graduated Magna Cum Laude. Together they began their practice in Tulsa, Oklahoma. Keeping the passion alive to help the hopeless, he has developed equipment for children with special needs as well as individuals with incurable and chronic problems.

With his wife, Dr. Mary, Dr. Marshall started Hands of Care, Inc., a non-profit organization that provides specialized care for special-needs children. Currently the Marshalls practice in Owasso, Oklahoma and have been blessed with four sons.

His passion, along with his wife and family, is to see those who are sick and hurting be healed, made whole and find their purpose in life.

Dr. Ray can be reached online at marshallspinalcare.com.

Made in the USA
San Bernardino, CA
20 June 2015